Lexile:

AR BL: 12/16
AR Pts:

Published in 2016 by Enslow Publishing, LLC
101 W. 23rd Street, Suite 240, New York, NY 10011

Library of Congress Cataloging-in-Publication Data

Newton, David E.
    Overpopulation : 7 billion people and counting / David E. Newton.
        pages cm. — (The end of life as we know it)
    Audience: Grade 7 to 8.
    Includes bibliographical references and index.
        ISBN 978-0-7660-7312-8
    1. Overpopulation—Juvenile literature. 2. Overpopulation—Economic aspects—Juvenile literature. I. Title.
    HB883.N4896 2016
    363.9'1—dc23
                            2015029189

Printed in the United States of America

To Our Readers: We have done our best to make sure all website addresses in this book were active and appropriate when we went to press. However, the author and the publisher have no control over and assume no liability for the material available on those websites or on any websites they may link to. Any comments or suggestions can be sent by e-mail to customerservice@enslow.com.

Portions of this book originally appeared in the book *Population: Too Many People?*

Photo Credits: Cover, TonyV3112/Shutterstock.com (busy street in China); p. 4 DIBYANGSHU SARKAR/AFP/Getty Images; p. 12 Gwoeii/Shutterstock.com; p. 19 BEN SIMON/AFP/Getty Images; p. 22 London News/Hulton Archive/Getty Images; p. 26 John Moore/Getty Images News/Getty Images; p. 32 AHMAD AL-RUBAYE/AFP/Getty Images; p. 36 ISSOUF SANOGO/AFP/Getty Images; p. 41 Ute Grabowsky/Photothek/Getty Images; p. 44 Edwin Levick/Hulton Archive/Getty Images; p. 49 Kzenon/Shutterstock.com; p. 54 Fairfax Media/Getty Images; p. 58 cdrin/Shutterstock.com; p. 61 Hulton Archive/Getty Images; p. 64 Tony Avelar/The Christian Science Monitor/Getty Images; p. 68 National Archive/Newsmakers/Hulton ArchivesGetty Images; p. 71 James D. Wilson/ Hulton Archive/Getty Images; p. 73 Sunny Forest/Shutterstock.com; p. 78 iStock.com/gionnixxx; p. 82 Dmitrijs Dmitrijevs/Shutterstock.com; p. 85 oliveromg/Shutterstock.com; p. 89 Alex Wong/ Newsmakers/Hulton Archive/Getty Images; p. 92 sima/Shutterstock.com; p. 96 Dirk Ercken/ Shutterstock.com; p. 101 Everett Historical/Shutterstock.com; pp. 103, 117 JAY DIRECTO/AFP/ Getty Images; p. 109 Mario Tama/Getty Images News/Getty Images; p. 115 PETER PARKS/AFP/Getty Images; p. 121 THIERRY CHARLIER/AFP/Getty Images; p. 124 Joe Raedle/Getty Images News/ Getty Images; p. 128 iStock.com/Natalia Pushchina; p. 131 Haacker/Fox Photos/Hulton Archive/Getty Images; p. 133 ChinaFotoPress/ChinaFotoPress/Getty Images.

CONTENTS

A crowd of people disembark from a train in India. That country is on track to become the most populated in the world in the next decade.

CHAPTER 1

THE POPULATION EXPLOSION

MONDAY, OCTOBER 31, 2011, WAS A VERY SPECIAL DAY for the Yadav family. On that day, a baby girl named Nargis was born to Vineeta and Ajay Yadav of Dhanaur village, outside of Lucknow, India.[1] But October 31, 2011, was also a very special day for the whole human family. According to world population experts, Baby Nargis was the seven billionth human on planet Earth. For better or worse, the human race had passed an important milestone.

DEMOGRAPHY: THE ART AND SCIENCE OF COUNTING PEOPLE

In fact, no one really knows if Nargis Yadav was the seven billionth human or not. Population experts chose just one of tens of thousands of babies born on that date to make a point: the rapid growth of the world population.

Demography, the study of human populations, is an inexact science. People are born, die, and move every day. No person or nation can know exactly how many people live in a country at any one time. And, few nations have the financial resources or care enough to count the number of people living within their borders carefully and on a regular basis. Even a developed nation like the United States makes an official count only once every ten years. Between these official censuses, authorities make educated guesses as to how many Americans there are.

Other nations count even less frequently or less efficiently. For example, the US Central Intelligence Agency (CIA) currently gives the population of Somalia as 10,428,043 for 2015. But that number is based on a census taken in 1975 and has not been officially updated since that time. Even that number is subject to doubt because of the large number of nomads, who are difficult to count, by the constant movement of refugees moving throughout the country, and because of the wars and other conflicts that have ravaged the nation for decades.[2]

Nor is Somalia unique in this respect. Experts have long argued about the true population of another African country, Nigeria. Current estimates range anywhere from 120 million to 200 million, depending on the source of the data. Some experts say the best estimate is somewhere in the middle, at about 186 million. But no one really knows for sure.[3]

GLOBAL POPULATION TRENDS

The important thing about Baby Nargis is what she stands for: human population that is growing faster and faster every year. Figure 1.1 makes that point dramatically. It shows the world's population from the beginning of the Christian era, 2000 years ago, to the present day. Notice how the world's population changed very little until around 1700 CE. It grew slowly but steadily during this time, increasing and decreasing over time but never reaching over 500 million.

Then, around 1700, a dramatic change began to occur. Notice on the graph how population began to increase; around 1850 it reached one billion, with two billion around 1930. That means it took about five million years, since the first humans appeared on Earth, for the first billion people to be born. But it took only eighty years for the next billion humans to arrive.

Figure 1.1

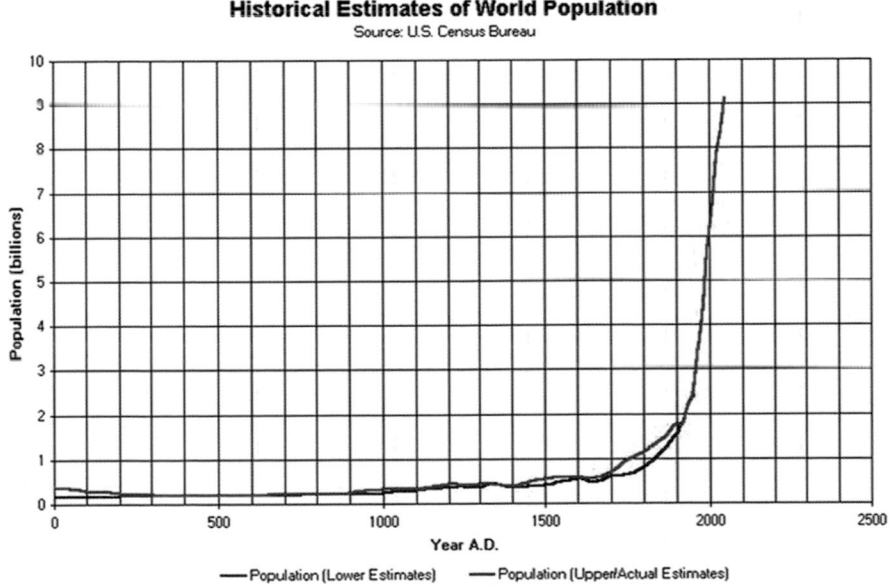

*Reprinted/made available with permission of Stevens Institute of Technology; © 2015 the Trustees of the Stevens Institute of Technology, Hoboken, NJ 07030

By 2015 world population was increasing at the rate of about seventy-seven million people annually. That is the equivalent of adding a country the size of Turkey each year.[4]

POPULATION TRENDS

Look at Figure 1.1. Follow the population line upward. The third billionth human was born in 1959, only thirty-three years after the second billionth. Number four billion came fifteen years later, in 1974, and number five billion, only thirteen years later, in 1987. Babies number six billion and seven billion arrived after a similar period of time, in 1999 and 2011, respectively. You can see that the story of human population since 1930 is very different from what went on before.

How should we feel about that fact? What, if anything, should we do about it? To answer questions like these, we need to understand the factors that affect population growth. Those factors include (1) how many children are born each year, (2) how many people die each year, and (3) how many people move in and out of a country. Chapter 2 describes the way in which these three factors work together to affect population change. Chapter 3 explains how changing death rates have had a major impact on population growth patterns.

Population changes in the United States and Canada are of special interest to most readers of this book. Chapter 4 outlines the most recent population data available for these two nations.

THE THREATS POSED BY POPULATION GROWTH

Was the news of Baby Nargis's birth a cause for celebration or mourning? Is a rapid rate of population growth a good or bad trend? Population experts do not agree.

The connection between population size and quality of life is very complex. In Chapter 5 you will read more about the views of people who think that population growth is bad and needs to be brought under control. Then Chapter 6 presents the position that population growth is desirable and should not be discouraged. Chapter 7 reviews the way each group feels about some important population-related issues in the world today.

TAKE ACTION!

What is the "population story" in the area where you live? Is population increasing? Decreasing? How fast is it changing? To find the answers to these questions, visit your local city hall, town hall, county clerk's office, or other governmental bureau that keeps population records for your area. Find out what population trends have been as far back as you can trace to the present day. Make a table or graph that summarizes the information you collect. Then create a Facebook page or website on which you can report your findings. Challenge readers to present their views about population trends in your area. How important are these trends to your friends, family, neighbors, and others who live in your area? Do they care about these trends? Should they care about them? What does your online page have to say about the importance of population issues in the region where you live?

FUTURE DIRECTIONS FOR POPULATION GROWTH

What about future population growth? Population predictions are always difficult to make. After all, there are a lot of things we don't know about the world's population today. So guessing what the future might be like is risky. But there is little doubt about one fact. Population growth is going to continue throughout your lifetime at a rate much like that of the last fifty years.

Experts predict that Baby Jones (or Baby Chan or Baby Rodriguez), the eighth billionth human, will arrive in about 2026, about the same time it took for baby number seven billion to arrive. That's only ten years away.

The one fact on which all population experts agree is that the world's population will continue to grow at a rapid rate for many decades.

What should the nations of the world do about this trend? Again, experts disagree. But when people discuss population growth today, they usually focus on birth rates. Improvements in health and medical practices have greatly reduced death rates in nearly all countries of the world. The movement of people in and out of nations is a relatively minor factor in population growth in most nations. So by far the factor that still makes the biggest difference in a nation's population is its birth rate.

Many nations today want to reduce their birth rates. They look into the future and see poverty, illness, misery, and early death for many of their people. They worry about depletion of resources and pollution. So they are trying a number of different methods for reducing the number of children born each year. India and China are examples of these countries.

Other nations would like to increase their birth rate. They believe that having more people will help them to better utilize their resources. For them, rising birth rates promise a better and brighter future for their country. Singapore is one example of nations with this philosophy.

This book is different from many that you may have already read, in that it explains and examines what experts and many nations face when they consider population questions. After reading the chapters which follow, you may think differently about the central question that we face: What can humans do to control out-of-control population growth rates around the world?

On our imaginary island of Kibo, the lakes are polluted and the cities are dirty and disease-ridden. Could overpopulation be to blame?

CHAPTER 2

MEASURING POPULATION TRENDS

PEOPLE WHO STUDY POPULATION TRENDS ARE CALLED demographers. Demography can sometimes be a challenging field of study. So we've arranged a special vacation that will help you understand the principles of demography with a minimum of pain and discomfort. We'll begin by boarding Fantasy Airlines Flight 232 for the island of Kibo. You won't find Kibo on any map. We have invented this tiny country in order to talk about some of the population issues nations face. Even though Kibo isn't real, the population problems we will describe are both real and typical of nations around the world.

After we arrive in Kibo, we discover the nation is experiencing some serious social problems. For example, its once crystal-clear lakes are now murky and smelly. Parts of Geo, the capital city, are crowded, dirty, and overrun with disease. Every morning and afternoon, Geo's air becomes smelly, hazy, and irritating to breathe. This is hardly the island paradise that Kibo was when it became a nation thirty years ago. What has happened to bring about this change?

Some people in government think the reason is that the island's population has grown too fast. They believe that the return of pure air and water and an improved standard of living will come only with a reduction in population growth. They have hired Kibo University's only demographer to advise them on this question. Here is what the demographer has to say.

THE POPULATION EQUATION

The basic ideas of population change are simple. If you want to predict a nation's population next year, you only have to know five facts:

1. Its population now.

2. How many children will be born in the next year. To demographers the number of children born per 1,000 people is the crude birth rate (CBR). They often use a second measure known as total fertility rate (TFR). Total fertility rate is the average number of children that would be born alive to a woman during her lifetime.

3. How many people will die in the next year.

4. How many people will move into—or immigrate to—the nation in the next year.

5. How many people will move out of—or emigrate from—the nation in the next year.

Then you can predict next year's population from the following "population equation:"

$$\begin{matrix} \textbf{population} \\ \textbf{next year} \end{matrix} = \begin{matrix} \text{population} \\ \text{now} \end{matrix} + \begin{matrix} \text{number of} \\ \text{births} \end{matrix} - \begin{matrix} \text{number of} \\ \text{deaths} \end{matrix} + \begin{matrix} \text{number of} \\ \text{immigrants} \end{matrix} - \begin{matrix} \text{number of} \\ \text{emigrants} \end{matrix}$$

No one knows what the exact number of births, deaths, immigrants, and emigrants will be next year. But demographers can often make a good guess by using the numbers from this year or last year.

For example, Kibo has a population this year of one hundred thousand. Last year, five thousand babies were born, two thousand people died, one hundred people moved into the country, and two hundred moved out. From this, demographers can predict that the population of Kibo next year will be:

$$\underset{\substack{\text{last year's} \\ \text{population}}}{100{,}000} + \underset{\substack{\text{number} \\ \text{of births}}}{5{,}000} - \underset{\substack{\text{number} \\ \text{of deaths}}}{2{,}000} + \underset{\substack{\text{number} \\ \text{of immigrants}}}{100} - \underset{\substack{\text{number} \\ \text{of emigrants}}}{200} = \underset{\substack{\text{this year's} \\ \text{population}}}{102{,}900}$$

That is, Kibo's population will increase by 2,900 over this year. A common measure used by demographers in talking about population growth is growth rate. Growth rate is the increase or decrease in a population compared to a base population. So:

$$\begin{matrix} \text{population growth rate} \end{matrix} = \begin{matrix} \text{increase or decrease} \\ \text{in population} \end{matrix} \div \begin{matrix} \text{base population} \\ \text{growth rate} \end{matrix} \times 100\%$$

For Kibo, the growth rate is 2,900.

$$\text{population growth rate} = 2{,}900 \div 100{,}000 \times 100\% = 2.9\%$$

HOW DEMOGRAPHY HELPS

At this point, the Prime Minister of Kibo interrupts the demographer:

Do we really need to go through all this? I don't much like mathematics. I just want to know what we have to do about our population problems!

The demographer replies:

For better or worse, you do need to understand basic mathematical concepts about demography. Let me show you why. Suppose you have decided that population growth is the cause of many of our nation's social problems. You think that a population increase of 2,900 per year is too much. You would like to see the nation's population level off, perhaps at about 125,000. To achieve that goal, you might decide to cut back on the growth rate. Since 2.9% seems too high, it should be cut back to 2.5% or 2.0%. Would one of these two choices solve your population problems?

A graph will answer that question for you. Notice that this graph (Figure 2.1) has three lines: one dotted, one solid, and one broken. The

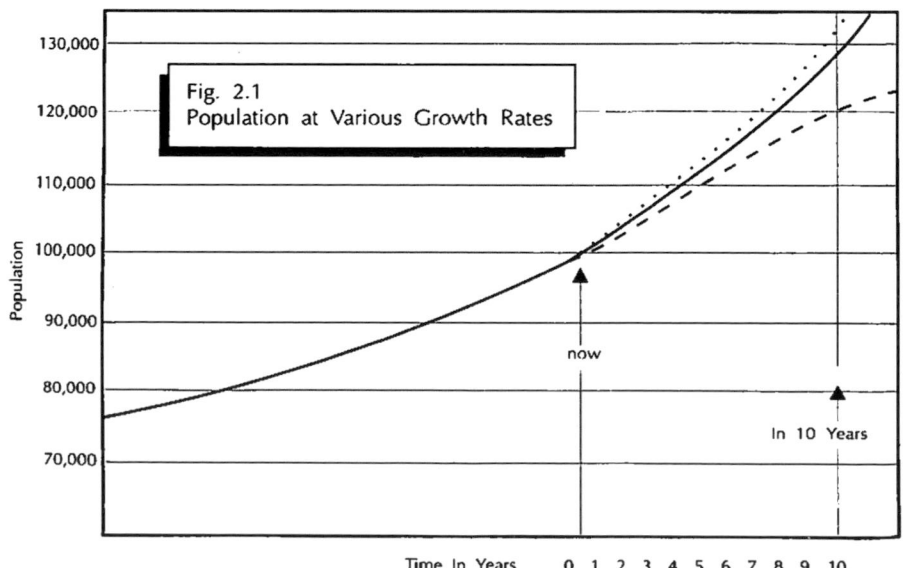

Fig. 2.1
Population at Various Growth Rates

dotted line shows what the nation's population will be over the next ten years at its present growth rate of 2.9%. The solid line shows what happens if you cut the growth rate back to 2.5%. And the broken line shows population trends with a 2.0% growth rate.

Notice that in all of these cases, the population continues to grow. It doesn't grow as fast at 2.5% or 2.0%, but it still grows.

The point to remember is this. No matter which growth rate you pick, Kibo will have a population of around 120,000 in less than ten years. And the population is going to continue to grow beyond that number in following years. You see, trying to cut back on population increase is very difficult, even if you cut back on the growth rate by a large amount.

PAYING FOR PROGRESS

The Prime Minister is amazed:

How did we get into this situation? No one in government ever decided that larger populations were a good thing for the country. In fact, I don't think anyone thought much about population issues until recently. Then, pollution, poverty, hunger, and a shortage of natural resources made some of us wonder about the nation's population. Suppose population increase is at the bottom of these problems. How did we get into this mess?

The demographer replies:

I have a surprise for you. Your government's successes in the past fifty years are the main reason for your current population worries. Here's the reason: Look back at the population equation. Here in Kibo, immigration and emigration do not play a very big part in that equation. Kibo is like most of the world's nations in that respect. Its population changes are related mostly to births and deaths.

Fifty years ago Kibo was a fairly primitive nation. The island did not have very good health or medical care. Many babies died shortly after birth, and mothers often died during childbirth. Epidemics and plagues were common. People didn't know very much about infections and diseases, so people often died young of pneumonia, smallpox, diphtheria, and other infections. In those days, the population equation for Kibo might have looked like this:

$$
\underset{\substack{\text{population} \\ \text{in 1930}}}{100{,}000} = \underset{\substack{\text{population} \\ \text{in 1929}}}{100{,}000} + \underset{\substack{\text{number} \\ \text{of births}}}{5{,}000} - \underset{\substack{\text{number} \\ \text{of deaths}}}{5{,}000}
$$

(We have left out immigration and emigration as factors because the numbers are so small in Kibo.)

Notice that the number of deaths was quite large. In fact, as many people died in 1929 as were born in that year. So the population stayed pretty much the same in 1930 as it was in 1929.

Until the mid-nineteenth century, most nations of the world had a similar population equation. Their populations might increase one year and decrease the next. But they did not increase or decrease dramatically over long periods of time.

But something happened in Kibo in 1930. People began to learn about modern health and medical practices. They discovered how to reduce infant deaths and deaths of mothers. They also learned how to fight infectious diseases and keep people alive longer. Kibo's death rate tumbled.

As the citizens of Kibo continued using modern health and medical practices, the number of deaths became smaller and smaller each year. Eventually, it got to the point shown in the population equation above, two thousand per year. So the answer to your question is an easy one. Population is increasing in Kibo today because the death rate is much smaller now than it was fifty years ago. The birth rate has not changed at all.

THE DEMOGRAPHIC TRANSITION

Kibo is now in the second stage of what population experts call the demographic transition. The term *demographic transition* refers to the stages a nation goes through as it adopts improved health techniques. Stage one of the demographic transition was described above. In that stage, birth rates and death rates are high and the nation's population remains stable.

In stage two, death rates fall because of improved health and medical practices. But birth rates don't change much. As a result, a country's

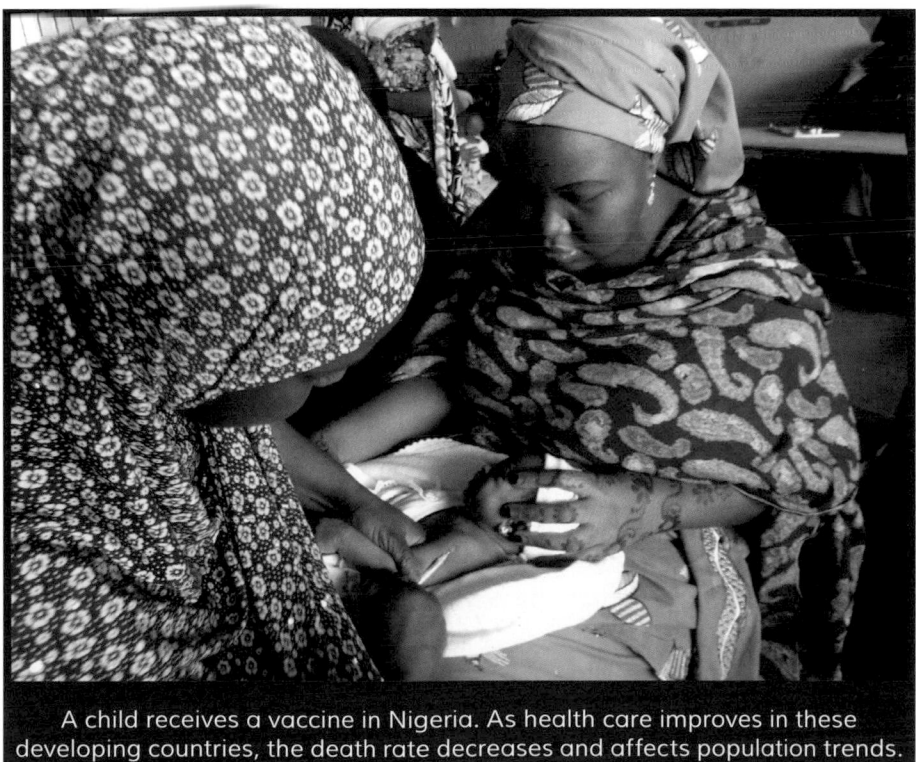

A child receives a vaccine in Nigeria. As health care improves in these developing countries, the death rate decreases and affects population trends.

growth rate goes up. The country experiences a fairly large population increase every year, just as Kibo is doing now.

But the demographic transition does not end at stage two. It *can't* end at this stage. No country can continue to have a growth rate of 2%, 3%, or 4% forever and survive as a nation. Consider just one example.

Nigeria had a population of ninety million in 1990. Its growth rate then was 3.0%. If Nigeria continued to grow at that rate in the future, it would have a population of 128 million in the year 2000, 231 million twenty years later, and nearly two billion within one hundred years. At that rate, Nigeria would soon have as many people as there are in China today! Of course, that seems unlikely to happen. Nigeria can't get "stuck" in the second stage forever. Instead, something will happen there, as it will in any other nation in stage two. That "something" is usually a decrease in birth rates.

Suppose Kibo could reduce the number of births next year to two thousand. Then the number of births would equal the number of deaths. There would be almost no population change. Kibo would have reached the third stage of the demographic transition. In this stage, both the number of births and the number of deaths is low. Living conditions are better because of improved health practices. But a lowered birth rate means that the population has become stable, that is, it is no longer increasing each year.

But suppose a nation decides not to (or can't) reduce its birth rate. Then the population continues to increase. At some point, however, nature takes over. It's unlikely that any nation in the world has enough natural resources to care for an unlimited number of people. Nigeria certainly does not have enough food, fuel, cotton, and other natural resources to support a population of five billion.

At that point, then, people begin dying of starvation, of illness, or of other causes. The death rate starts rising again. Eventually it gets to be as high as the birth rate. Population increase comes to a halt. The nation—with a high birth *and* death rate—has returned to stage one of the demographic transition.

The term *more developed countries* (MDCs) refers to those nations that have a relatively high standard of living. Today, most MDCs are in the third state of the demographic transition. They have low birth and death rates and stable population growth.

Less developed countries (LDCs) refers to those nations with relatively lower standards of living. Most LDCs of the world are in the second stage of the demographic transition. They have low death rates but still have high birth rates. Their populations are continuing to grow at a rapid rate.

IMMIGRATION AND EMIGRATION

Another factor affecting population growth is migration. The term *migration* refers to the movement of people from one place to another. Emigrants are people who migrate out of a region. Immigrants are people who migrate into an area.

Migration can occur within a single nation—for example, in Canada from Vancouver to Toronto—or across national boundaries—for example, from Vancouver to Seattle in the United States. Migration does not have the same kinds of effect on population that births and deaths do. Births and deaths occur all the time in every nation of the world. But migration can have very large or very small effects on a nation's population. In Japan today, for example, the number of people who move into and out of the nation is very small compared to Japan's overall population.

Irish emigrants sail for the United States during the potato famine of the 1840s. Ireland lost 10 percent of its population because of the high death rate and people leaving the country.

A classic example of the dramatic effects that migration can have on a nation's population occurred in Ireland during the eighteenth century. Potato blight—a disease that killed the island's major food crop—swept through the nation between 1845 and 1849.

During that period of time, 750,000 Irish—about 10% of the nation's population—died of starvation and related diseases. Another million left their homeland to move to other countries; the vast majority migrated to the United States. By 1900 continued migration had reduced Ireland's population by nearly half, to its 1780 level of just over four million.

INTERNAL MIGRATION

People are constantly on the move *within* nations also. For example, in some LDCs, families change their campsites every day or every week.

They must keep moving in order to find food, water, and fuel. People in MDCs often lead a kind of nomadic lifestyle, too, although not for the same reasons. The US Census Bureau has estimated, for example, that the average American moves 11.7 times during his or her lifetime.[1]

For nearly a century, the most common form of internal migration has been the movement of people from rural areas to cities. Only 150 years ago, every society in the world was primarily a rural society. People made their living on farms and by hunting. Urban areas were an unimportant part of their lives. In 1900 only Great Britain, of all nations in the world, had a larger urban than rural population.[2]

That situation changed dramatically in the twentieth century. Migration patterns within the United States are similar to those that exist elsewhere in the world, so we can use it to illustrate the patterns. For example, in 1700, only two out of every hundred Americans lived in an urban area. By 1800, that number had increased, barely, to five out of one hundred. Then, beginning about 1825, migration from farms to cities began in earnest.

The table in Figure 2.2 shows how urban population increased during the nineteenth and twentieth centuries. Notice that the rural population in the United States has dropped from about 95 percent shortly after the country's founding to just under 20 percent in 2010.

Today, migration to urban areas has become the rule in most countries of the world. In 1900, only 3% of the world's population lived in cities. But by 2015, for the first time in history, more people lived in urban areas than in rural areas. At that point, urban population was growing at just over 1.8 percent per year.

At first, urbanization in LDCs took place more slowly than it did in MDCs. But that pattern changed in the early 1970s. Now, people in LDCs

YEAR	URBAN[1]	PERCENT	RURAL[1]	PERCENT
1790	202	5	3,728	95
1800	322	6	4,986	94
1810	525	7	6,714	93
1820	693	7	8,945	93
1830	1,127	9	11,739	91
1840	1,845	11	15,224	89
1850	3,544	15	19,648	85
1860	6,217	20	25,227	80
1870	9,902	26	28,656	74
1880	14,130	29	36,026	71
1890	22,106	35	40,841	65
1900	30,160	40	45,835	60
1910	41,999	46	49,973	54
1920	54,158	51	51,553	49
1930	68,955	56	53,820	44
1940	74,424	57	57,246	43
1950[2]	96,468	64	54,230	36
1960	125,269	70	54,054	30
1970	149,325	73	53,887	27
1980	169,431	75	57,115	25
1988	189,413	77	56,339	23

Figure 2.2

Urban and Rural Population in the United States, (1790-1988)

[1] In thousands

[2] New definitions of urban and rural areas used beginning in 1950. Folllow data using 1950 definition.

are moving to cities even faster than they are in MDCs. In its 2014 report, "World Urbanization Prospects," the United Nations reported that 48 percent of the world's less developed regions had become urbanized compared to 35 percent only fifteen years earlier. The report predicted that the rate of urbanization in LDCs would increase to 63 percent by 2050.

THE ATTRACTION OF CITIES

Why have masses of people throughout the world migrated to cities? The answer seems to be the same in both LDCs and MDCs. People everywhere tend to believe that jobs will be more readily available in cities; that education and health care will be better; that cultural and entertainment opportunities will be more abundant; and, in general, that the quality of life will be better than it is back home, "on the farm." It is easy for us to question that belief. Our image of slum life in almost any LDC makes us wonder if this is really a "better" life for people who live there. But the answer seems to be "yes" in most cases. For all the problems of urban living, rural life is often less healthful, more difficult, and less desirable for many people. In any case, vast numbers of rural-to-urban migrants around the world are continuing to choose cities over farms.

Chances are, therefore, that urban areas worldwide will continue to grow. As they do, the special problems created by crowded cities are likely to become more and more substantial. By the twenty-first century, many "population problems" are likely to be "crowded urban area problems."

THE DRIVERS OF MIGRATION

What are the forces that cause people to leave their homes and travel great distances to another part of their homeland or to an entirely new country? There are many possible answers to this question. For some cultures, moving one's home is simply a part of people's way of life. Nomads, for example, move from place to place primarily to keep up with the food supply on which they depend. One of the other drivers of migration is the desire to find a better way of life. Americans probably know that story as well as any other people in the world. The United States has been populated by people who came to improve their lives, whether they came from Great Britain, Italy, China, India, Mexico, or a hundred other nations around the world.

That pattern is as true in the 2010s as it was in the 1600s, when the first Pilgrims arrived on American shores. One of the great political battles of the twenty-first century, in fact, has centered on how the United States should deal with the thousands and thousands of immigrants from Mexico and South and Central America. Should we open our arms to them, like the Statue of Liberty, welcoming them to a land where they will find better opportunities? Or should we place restrictions on the number of people who come here, the types of jobs they can hold, the family members whom they may be joining, or other criteria? As the number of illegal immigrants to the United States begins to exceed ten million, that question becomes an ever more serious political, social, economic, and humanitarian issue.

Immigrants are often willing take great chances in the hopes of a better life in a new place. Here, US Border patrol agents arrest undocumented Mexican immigrants attempting to enter the United States.

A HOT TOPIC: IMMIGRATION

Today, illegal immigration is an issue of considerable debate in the United States. Many people enter the country illegally because they hope that they will be able to make a safer, happier, more prosperous life than they could have in their native country. Some Americans believe that the United States should welcome these immigrants with open arms. After all, they say, almost every American is an immigrant or has immigrants in their family history. This nation, above all others, should be welcoming to those in need.

Many other people disagree. They say that anyone who wants to enter the United States should follow legal procedures. Americans should not be forced to pay for housing, feeding, educating, and providing jobs for people who came here illegally. What do you think?

Another driver of immigration is despair about the ability to survive in one's homeland. Many people who cross into the United States from the south, for example, come not primarily in the hopes of finding a better life. They may be fleeing living conditions in their native lands that they believe they cannot survive. Stories abound of men, women, and children who leave Honduras, Guatemala, El Salvador, and other Central American countries because society has broken down there, and roving gangs are likely to kill any innocent person for any reason at any time. Individuals who live in such circumstances sometimes see no other choice than to immigrate to a country where life can be at least somewhat safer.

Such immigration patterns are by no means limited to the United States. In its 2014 report, "World at War," the United Nations High Commissioner for Refugees (UNHCR) estimated that 59.5 million people worldwide had been displaced from their homeland because of a surge in war, conflict, and persecution of various kinds. For example, citizens of Iraq and Syria fled conflict in their nations into the neighboring countries of Lebanon, Jordan, and Turkey in the tens and hundreds of thousands. Similar scenes were seen in other war-torn areas, such as Yemen, Burundi, South Sudan, Republic of the Congo, Nigeria, Mali, and Central African Republic.[4]

People flee their native lands not only because of war and civil conflict, but also because of persecution on the basis of their race, religion, or some other characteristic. In Myanmar, for example, the majority Buddhist population is strongly antagonistic toward the minority Muslim Rohingya population, who are forced to live in conditions similar to the apartheid society that existed for so long in South Africa. UNHCR estimated that more than fifty thousand Rohingya attempted to escape Myanmar in 2014 alone, of whom nearly a thousand were known to have perished at sea while attempting to reach a new land. In many instances, the countries to which the Rohingya fled refused them asylum, and they were returned to the seas on which they arrived.[5]

ILLEGAL IMMIGRATION

People who decide to emigrate from one country to another country sometimes do so without following the laws for such actions. They do not apply for visas, present themselves at a border crossing, or take the other steps that legal immigrants follow when they enter a new country. Illegal immigration, in general, is relatively uncommon. But there are times and places where very large numbers of people emigrate to another country illegally.

According to the Pew Research Center, for example, there were 11.2 million illegal immigrants in the United States in 2014, about 3.5 percent of the nation's population. Just over half of those illegal immigrants (52 percent) came from one country, Mexico. Another 15 percent came from Central America, including El Salvador, Guatemala, and Honduras. Much smaller numbers came from Asian countries, such as India, China, and the Philippines.[6,7]

TAKE ACTION!

Reading this book will help you become knowledgeable about population issues. But how knowledgeable are other members of your family? Friends and acquaintances? Other members of the community? Design an experiment to answer those questions. Start by making a list of factual questions you think are important about population issues, such as:

- How large do you think the world population is?

- How fast is the world's population growing? For example, how long before the world will add another billion people?

- What are the five most populous countries in the world?

- What are the factors that make a country's population grow or decline?

Next, add some questions about people's opinions and attitudes, such as:

- How important do you think population issues are? For example, how often do you talk with others about population issues in the world?

- What problems do you think population growth causes for Americans?

(continued on next page)

(continued from previous page)

- What actions, if any, do you think need to be taken in the United States to deal with population issues?

You will be able to think of other questions about population also. When you have a list of about fifteen questions, make a list of people of whom you want to ask those questions. Then prepare a report that summarizes what you found out in your experiment. Think of an interesting way to report these results to other people, such as a "news flash" handout you can give to people or a Facebook page that summarizes your results and lets people respond to the information you learned in your study.

CHAPTER 3

THE DEMOGRAPHIC TRANSITION

KIBO'S STORY IS NOT ALL THAT DIFFERENT FROM THAT of many nations. The twenty nations with the highest growth rate in the world in 2014 (all in Africa and the Middle East) have growth rates of more than 2%.[1] The issues these nations face today would sound familiar to the government of Kibo.

An important factor in the world's population crisis is the reduction in death rates that has taken place over the past century. How did that reduction come about? Besides natural causes of death (old age), people die in large numbers as the result of three major factors: war, famine, and disease. Of these three, war and famine can have dramatic and short-lived effects on a nation's population.

In Baghdad, Iraqis carry the coffins of civilians killed by Al-Qaeda.
The country has lost a large portion of its population to recent wars.

WAR AND CIVIL CONFLICT

World War I illustrates the devastating effects of war. Between 1914 and 1918, Germany lost 1.6 million soldiers, about three percent of its population. In the same war France lost 1.3 million (3.2% of its population), Austro-Hungary 1.25 million (2.5%), and Romania 335,000 (2.5%).[2]

Civilians are victims of warfare, too. When Genghis Khan attacked China in the early thirteenth century, for example, he destroyed a large part of the Chinese population. According to one estimate, the invading Mongols killed thirty-five million civilians—an astounding 30% of the population—in a single decade.[3]

Many of the victims of World War II were civilians. About 60% of the twenty-five million Soviets killed in that war were civilians. All told, the war accounted for the death of one in every three Soviets who had been alive in 1935.[4]

In recent times, regional wars have sometimes had dramatic, if also short-lived, effects on population. The Iran-Iraq war of 1980–1988 is an example. During this conflict, between one and two million soldiers and civilians were killed on both sides. That means that at least 2% of Iran's population and perhaps as much as 5% of Iraq's was lost during the war.[5]

HUNGER AND FAMINE

Famine can have similar effects on a nation's population. Throughout history, the Asian continent has been especially devastated by famines. In the two thousand years prior to 1911, for example, 1,828 famines were recorded in China.[6] Most of these famines affected only one region of the nation, but many did spread across the country. Imagine living in a land that almost every year has a serious famine that kills hundreds of thousands of people.

The situation has not been much better in India. One authority estimates that nineteen million Indians died as a result of famine in just ten years, between 1891 and 1901.[7]

A variety of conditions can bring about famine. Rain, drought, insects, or wars can all destroy crops. Without enough food, people can starve to death in large numbers.

Events in Ethiopia and particularly the Sudan in the 1980s illustrate the many possible causes of famine. Over a five-year period, more than a million people may have starved to death in these two nations.[8] One reason for this disaster was weather. Years of unusually dry weather had reduced crop yields in both nations. But other factors were involved. National and international authorities agreed, for example, that, in spite of unfavorable weather conditions, Sudan had enough food in 1988 to feed all its people. The problem was in getting the food to the people who needed it.

One part of that problem was the nation's transportation system. Sudanese roads and railroads are primitive and heavy rains made both unusable. Southern Sudan, where famine was worst, had few airports. Also, the Sudanese government was relatively inefficient. Food stored in the capital of Khartoum had a way of "disappearing" for months before reappearing on a railway siding or in a warehouse far from its intended destination.

Finally, rebels in southern Sudan had been carrying on a war against the central government for more than three years. The federal government was reluctant to supply food to people in its rebellious southern provinces. Whatever the causes, the effects of the famine were familiar. At least half a million Sudanese died of starvation.[9]

This brief analysis should remind us how complex famines can be. Simply shipping tons of food to starving people will not always—and in this case, did not—relieve their misery.

DISEASE

Wars and famines come and go. One cause of death, however, is ever present. It threatens all human societies at all times. It is the single most important reason that humans die prematurely. That factor is disease.

The term *disease* covers a number of life-threatening conditions. Some are inborn problems caused by hereditary factors. Some forms of diabetes, for example, are genetic diseases or, more properly, genetic disorders.

Other diseases are caused by improper diet. Nutritional diseases occur when a person does not receive adequate amounts of some essential nutrient in his or her diet. Kwashiorkor, for example, which is found most often in children, occurs when a person lacks sufficient protein in his or her diet. The disease usually develops after the age of one year when the child has stopped taking mother's milk and begins to eat a diet high in grains. These grains meet the child's energy needs, but they lack the protein needed for body development. The most prominent characteristics of kwashiorkor is a bloated stomach. If the disease is left untreated, the child is likely to develop diarrhea, lose his or her appetite, become apathetic, and eventually die of protein starvation.

A third category of disease is infectious diseases, which are transmitted from one person to another by some agent, such as a bacterium, virus, worm, or some other organism. One of the best known examples of an

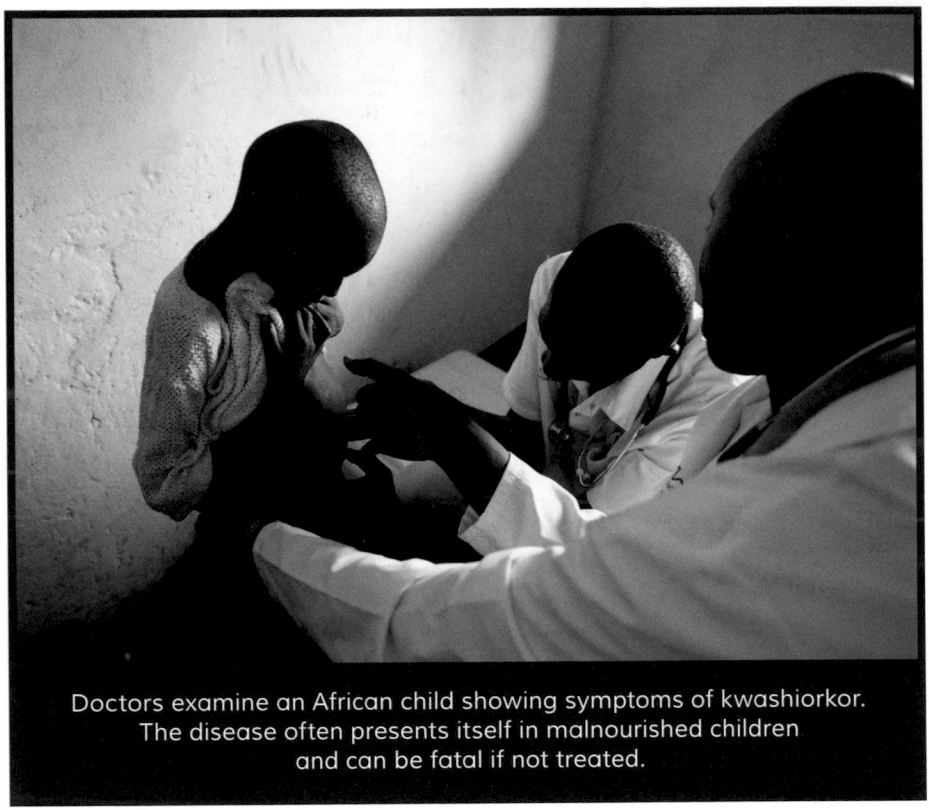

Doctors examine an African child showing symptoms of kwashiorkor.
The disease often presents itself in malnourished children
and can be fatal if not treated.

infectious disease today is acquired immunodeficiency syndrome (AIDS).
AIDS is caused by a virus known as the human immunodeficiency virus
(HIV). HIV is transmitted from one person to another by means of bodily
fluids, primarily blood and semen.

THE SCOURGE OF EPIDEMICS

Occasionally an infectious disease spreads through a community, killing
a large number of people. Such an event is known as an epidemic. Perhaps
the best-known epidemic in human history was the Black Death of the
fourteenth century. Black Death is another name for bubonic plague, a
disease caused by the bacterium *Pasteurella pestis*. Plague first appeared

in Europe during the sixth century and then again eight centuries later. Experts believe that the disease probably spread to Europe from China. It struck first on the European continent in Constantinople (modern Istanbul) in 1347.

Within three years, the plague had spread throughout the continent— as far west as Portugal and Ireland, as far north as Sweden and Russia, and as far south as the Mediterranean Sea. Over the next three decades, it died out and reappeared several times in most parts of Europe.

No one can be sure of the number of people who died of plague. But experts agree that it was the most devastating disaster to strike Europe in recorded history. About a quarter of the continent's population died out during the first sweep through the area. And another 15% probably died by the end of the century.[10] Figure 3.1 gives an idea of the epidemic's effect on the European population.

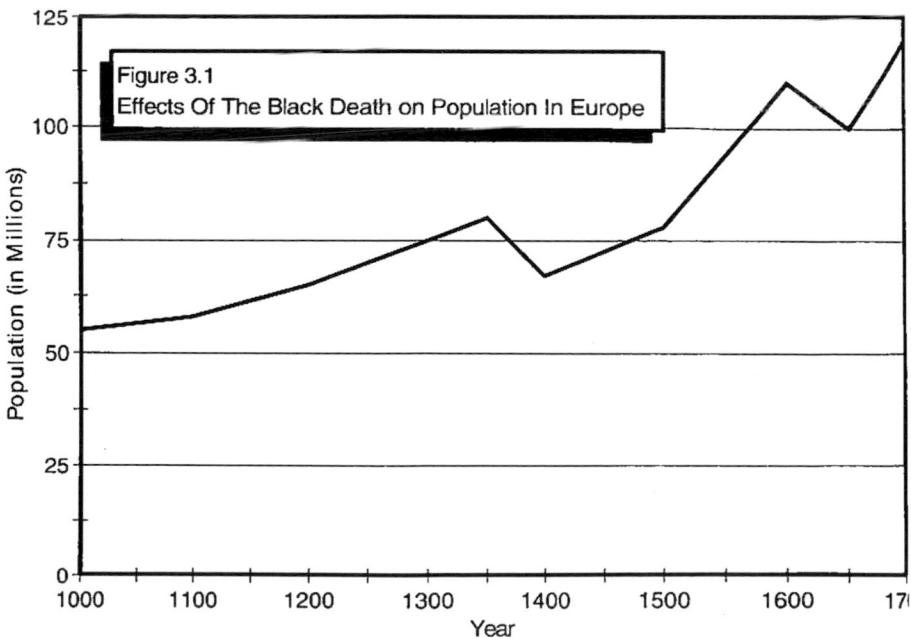

Figure 3.1
Effects Of The Black Death on Population In Europe

Perhaps the most troublesome epidemic of modern times has been the HIV/AIDS epidemic. That epidemic began in the late 1980s when a handful of gay men came down with medical problems that were almost never seen in their demographic group. Medical workers were baffled as to the nature of the disease, and gay men (primarily) began dying from the disease, which appeared to have no cure. By 1987 about 15,000 individuals had died in the United States of the disease, a number that continued to rise rapidly over the next decade, until it reached more than 50,000 per year in 1995. At that point, drugs became available to treat the HIV/AIDS disease, and the death rate in the United States began to drop

TAKE ACTION!

What are the most serious demographic problems that less developed nations have to deal with today? To answer this question, select one specific LCD to study in more detail. You can choose a country from the list of the forty-eight nations designated by the United Nations in 2015 as the "least developed nations in the world."

Go online to see what you can find out about the health problems faced by the country you have chosen to study. What factor or factors contribute to the population problems that nation faces? How could the United States government or individual American citizens (like yourself) help this nation to overcome its health problems? Prepare a list of specific actions someone in your own community could take to help the nation you are studying, such as contributing to international health agencies, lobbying the US government, or making contact with young adults in the country you are studying. Think of a method for letting other people in your community (or beyond your community) find out what you have learned about the health and population problems in the nation you have studied.

off. By 2010 it had fallen back to about 10,000 per year, a number that included primarily gay men and IV drug users.[11]

The nature of the HIV/AIDS epidemic has been quite different in other parts of the world, where heterosexual women and men are the most likely individuals to contract the disease. In many regions that are too poor to afford the medications with which HIV/AIDS can be treated, death rates remain high. In 2015 the World Health Organization (WHO) estimated that about thirty-five million people worldwide were infected with the HIV virus, of whom only about a third were receiving treatment. An estimated 1.5 million people had died of the disease in 2013, and a total of about thirty-nine million people are thought to have died since the disease first appeared twenty-five years earlier. Sub-Saharan Africa was home to the largest fraction of HIV/AIDS cases, about 70 percent of the total reported every year.[12]

THE CONQUEST OF DISEASE

The biggest population story of the last hundred years has been the conquest of disease. Scientists have learned a great deal about the ways to prevent and cure many types of disease. Thus, millions of people who would have died of disease a century ago are more likely to live to old age. The four most effective tools in the conquest of disease have been: (1) improved knowledge about nutrition; (2) vaccinations; (3) better public health practices; and (4) development of new medicines.

Nutrition

In 2013 a baby born in Singapore was more than fifty-three times more likely to live to the age of one year as a baby born in Afghanistan.[13] The major reason for this large difference in survival rate is nutrition. When young children get enough of the right kinds of food, they are likely to live to be adults.

Today, nations around the world know what constitutes proper nutrition for both young children and adults. Unfortunately, many LDCs lack money, skilled workers, and public education that would enable them to use the knowledge about nutrition they already have. As a result, infant death rates and, therefore, overall death rates remain high in many LDCs.

Vaccinations

As far back as 1800, scientists knew that vaccinations could protect people from infectious disease. Use of that knowledge has reduced the rates of influenza, tuberculosis, yellow fever, measles, rubella, poliomyelitis, diphtheria, tetanus, mumps, and whooping cough in MDCs. Again, lack of resources has prevented many LDCs from making similar use of vaccinations to reduce the rate of infectious disease and, hence, death rates in their nations. In addition, vaccines are still not available for some diseases—malaria is the most obvious example—that are of greatest concern in LDCs.

Public Health Practices

The germ theory of disease, proposed by Louis Pasteur in the 1870s, clearly demonstrated that a person's health is also a community problem. Sewage dumped into a public water supply can cause disease throughout a community. With this understanding arose the science of public health. Today, public health measures such as waste treatment, water purification,

A major factor in reducing death rates in many populations has been improved public health, such as efforts to clean up the water supply. This photo shows a boy in Mozambique washing his hands from a local water tap.

vaccination, and nutritional education are common in MDCs. However, even the most basic public health measures are still absent in many parts of the developing world. As a result, disease continues to spread and cause high death rates in many LDCs.

New Medicines

Finally, disease is less of a problem in MDCs because medical science has invented a whole range of new medicines with which to treat everything from gunshot wound infections and minor cuts to syphilis and pneumonia. People in MDCs who might once have died from such conditions are now saved rather easily with these new medicines. In many LDCs, new drugs and medicines are simply not available.

Death rates in MDCs have fallen largely because of improved health and medical knowledge and because of better health and medical practices based on that knowledge. Death rates in many LDCs remain high because the money, personnel, and facilities needed to put that knowledge into practice are not available.

Progress in medical science has, therefore, had an enormous effect on the populations of most nations of the world. Nearly everywhere death rates have declined, often dramatically. At the same time, birth rates—at least in the LDCs—have remained high. This combination of high birth rates and low death rates has led to skyrocketing populations in many nations throughout the world.

CHAPTER 4

POPULATION ISSUES IN NORTH AMERICA

THE STORY OF POPULATION IN NORTH AMERICA IS, to a large extent, a story of immigration. Less than one percent of the people living in the United States and Canada today can claim to be descended from truly native Americans. By native Americans, we mean people who have lived on this continent for many hundreds or thousands of years. These peoples were the only ones living in North America until the early 1600s.

No one really knows how many native Americans were living in North America when people began emigrating from Europe. Estimates range from a low of less than four million to a high of more than fifty million in 1492.[1]

One authority cites 220,000 as the most likely number of native Americans in Canada during the seventeenth century.[2] Whatever the exact number, native populations were, over the next three centuries, overwhelmed by immigrants from other parts of the world.

A photograph shows new immigrants to America looking at the Statue of Liberty in the 1910s. Most of the population of North America can be traced back to immigrants looking for a new life.

IMMIGRATION TO THE UNITED STATES

The first wave of immigrants to the United States began arriving in the early 1600s. Although no official count was made until 1820, experts estimate that up to a million people arrived from Europe during the colonial period.[3] Most came from England. The population of New England, Virginia, and Maryland was, by 1700, overwhelmingly English.

Smaller numbers came from other Northern European countries. Dutch settled in New York, Swedes along the Delaware River, and Germans in Pennsylvania, for example. But these non-English settlements were generally small, isolated, and restricted to specific parts of the country.

Immigrants traveled to the New World for a great variety of reasons. Some came to find religious freedom and others to escape unbearable poverty. But the great majority were probably not the "huddled masses" nor the "wretched refuse" described on the Statue of Liberty. They were, instead, "persons with at least a minimal economic and social standing" that they wanted to maintain in their adopted country.[4]

Many immigrants were looking for a way to improve their place in society. They often arrived as indentured servants who agreed to work for someone for four or five years in exchange for lodging and food—and the guarantee of freedom at the end of that period of time.

Black immigrants from Africa, on the other hand, were a different type of servant. They came as involuntary and permanent slaves with little or no hope of ever regaining their freedom. The first African slaves arrived in 1619. By the end of the century, a quarter million African men, women, and children had been transported to the United States. Their presence here soon eliminated the need for white indentured servants.

During the second wave of immigration, which began in the late eighteenth century and continued until the early 1920s, more than thirty-five million people entered the United States. An unknown, but relatively small, number of the second wave eventually returned to their native countries.

Figure 4.1 shows how this second wave of immigrants differed from the first. In many respects, the second wave of immigrants were similar to those of the first wave in the reasons why they came. Population growth in Southern and Eastern Europe made it more and more difficult for peasants and artisans to maintain their standard of living. They looked to the United States not necessarily as a way of becoming fabulously rich, but as a way of maintaining a decent lifestyle.

By the early 1900s, historically liberal attitudes toward immigration in the United States began to change. The general public was less and less willing to accept millions of "foreigners" every year. Congress began to pass a series of laws that greatly restricted the number and type of people who could enter the United States.

Laws enacted in 1921 and 1924 limited immigration to about 150,000 people per year and excluded certain nationalities and type of individuals. These laws were re-enacted as the McCarran-Walter Immigration Act of 1952, maintaining a generally restrictive immigration policy into the late twentieth century.

Immigration patterns also have changed dramatically in the past two decades. We are now seeing a flood of immigrants from Asia and South and Central America. The number of immigrants corning from Cambodia, for example, increased more than a hundredfold between 1960 and 1990, from 1,200 during the first decade of that period to more than 125,000 in the 1980s. Similarly, the number of Pakistani immigrants increased by 800% during that period, the number of Koreans by 700%, and the number of Laotians by 21,800%.[5]

Figure 4.1. Immigrants Coming to the United States

Country	1820-1849	1850-1879	1880-1909	1910-1939	1940-1979	1980-2009
Canada	48,457	506,120	618,263	1,820,704	947,208	530,358
Central America	448	784	8,374	39,043	158,895	2,502,572
China	43	313,241	100,949	57,438	38,968	530,582
France	122,324	189,617	151,544	128,938	134,042	96,464
Germany	515,913	2,451,565	2,353,025	678,327	905,924	255,101
India	80	258	3,375	6,105	22,252	731,925
Ireland	575,434	1,879,169	1,427,711	396,284	100,678	99,055
Mexico	14,091	10,536	34,327	716,988	771,829	4,418,222
Philippines	0	4	625	457	92,004	1,374,120
Russia	886	37,087	2,087,764	1,171,075	3,387	494,870
United Kingdom	309,258	1,556,758	1,186,177	776,453	547,716	443,674

Source: United States Department of Homeland Security. *Yearbook of Immigration Statistics: 2013.* Washington, DC: US Department of Homeland Security, Office of Immigration Statistics, 2014. Available online at http://www.dhs.gov/sites/default/files/publications/ois_yb_2013_0.pdf

IMMIGRATION PATTERNS

Figure 4.1 provides a great deal of information about immigration patterns in the United States over the past two hundred years. What does that information tell you about the ways in which immigration has affected the US population and how it might be affecting our population today?

Select a specific country to study in more detail, preferably one whose immigration patterns interest or puzzle you. What is it about the immigration data that is interesting or puzzling? How can you explain the patterns you see in this table? What do they tell you about population issues in the United States today? What forces might have caused people to leave their homeland in large numbers at various times in history?

IMMIGRATION TO CANADA

Canadian immigration patterns have been somewhat similar to those of the United States. The first English immigrants arrived in Nova Scotia in 1749, the first Germans in 1751, and the first Scots in 1779. Only in Quebec did non-British immigrants—the French—outnumber those from the United Kingdom.

The largest number of immigrants to Canada before the nineteenth century was from the United States. For example, at least 60% of the residents of Nova Scotia in 1755 had come originally from New England states. After 1780, more than 30,000 Loyalists also left the United States for Nova Scotia. Similar patterns existed in Quebec, Ontario, and, after 1782, New Brunswick.[6]

POPULATION CHANGES IN THE UNITED STATES

Immigration has undoubtedly played an important role in shaping the face of North America. But, as with all nations, the more important factor in determining population size and character is natural increase. The term *natural increase* refers to the excess of births over deaths in any one year. For example, if 10,000 people are born in one year in a state and 1,000 die, the natural increase for that state is 9,000.

The population of the United States grew very rapidly in its first century as a nation. The solid line in Figure 4.2 shows how the nation's population has changed since 1790. Notice how the population increased by about a third every ten years between 1790 and 1860.

The dotted line on the graph shows the rate of increase. Notice that between 1790 and 1940, the rate of population increase fell slowly. Then it picked up for two decades before beginning to drop back again. The

Figure 4.2

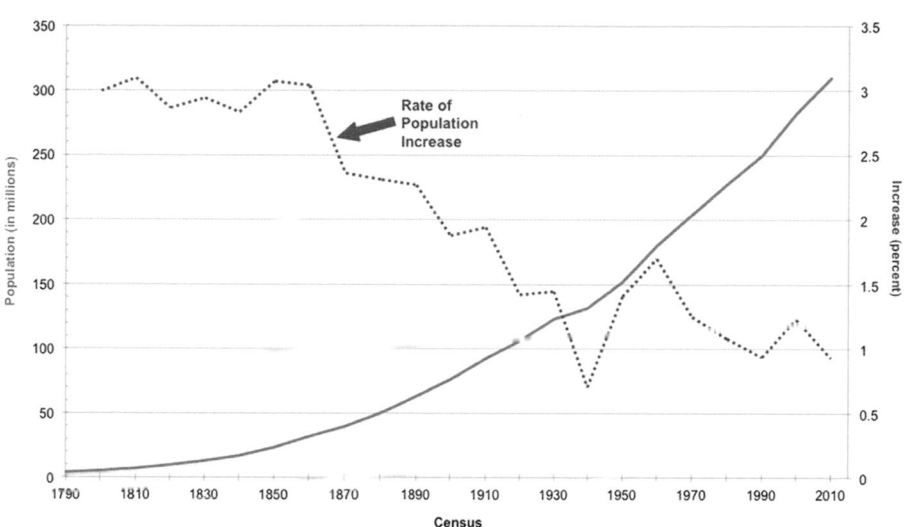

Population of the United States, 1790–2010

Rate of
Population
Increase

The racial makeup of the US population has become steadily more diverse over the past century.

spurt in growth rate after World War II is sometimes known as the Baby Boom. The major reasons for the changes shown in Figure 4.2 have been falling birth and death rates in the United States.

Population growth has not been uniform throughout the United States. At first, the greatest growth occurred along the Eastern seaboard. Over time, the population of the Midwest, South, and Far West began to grow. Older areas in the East began to experience much slower rates of growth.

The racial composition of the US population has also changed drastically in recent decades. For a hundred years, citizens were classified by the government as either "white" or "black." More recent censuses have tried to count other racial and ethnic groups, such as Native Americans,

Figure 4.3

YEAR	WHITE	BLACK	NATIVE AMERICAN	ASIAN	HISPANIC*	"OTHER"
1790	81%	19%				
1800	81%	19%				
1850	84%	16%				
1860	86%	14%				<1%
1870	87%	13%				<1%
1880	87%	13%				<1%
1890	88%	12%				<1%
1900	88%	12%				<1%
1910	89%	11%				<1%
1920	90%	10%				<1%
1930	90%	10%				<1%
1940	90%	10%				<1%
1950	89%	10%				1%
1960	89%	10%				1%
1970	88%	11%				1%
1980	86%	12%	0.6%	1.6%	6%	2%
1985	85%	12%	0.7%	2.3%	8%	3%
1990	80%	12%	0.8%	2.9%	9%	4%
2000	75%	12%	0.9%	3.8%	12.5%	5.5%
2010	72%	13%	0.9%	4.9%	16.3%	6.2%

Racial Constitution of US Population (1790–2010)[7]

*May be of any race.

Hispanics, and Asians. Figure 4.3 shows more recent data on the racial makeup of the US population.

The distribution of Americans between urban and rural settings has also shifted in the last century. Recall that the United States first became a more urban than rural nation in the very early 1900s.

POPULATION CHANGES IN CANADA

Most US population trends are reflected in Canadian data. Figure 4.4 shows Canada's population and rate of growth since its first census in 1867. The population of Newfoundland is included after 1949, the date of its admission to the confederation. Notice that the rate of population growth has been falling since the 1960s.

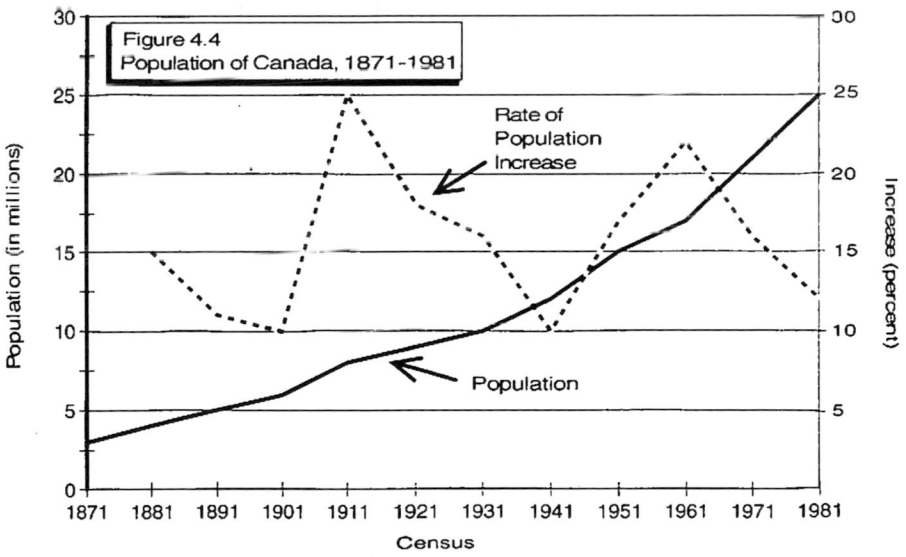

Figure 4.4
Population of Canada, 1871–1981

Population growth in the Canadian West has not matched that of the US West. Although the provinces of Alberta and British Columbia began to experience population explosions after World War II, Saskatchewan and Manitoba have recorded only modest population gains. As in the United States, population has shifted from rural to urban areas in Canada. In 1990 about three quarters of all Canadians lived in cities and towns rather than in rural areas.[8]

THE 2010 US CENSUS

The United States conducted its twenty-third decennial (ten-year) census in 2010. The official population set by the US Bureau of the Census, based on that survey, was 308,745,538. Some trends that are especially worthy of comment include the following topics.

Birth rate: The birth rate among American women was 13.0, less than the previous low of 14.0 recorded in 2009. (The estimated birth rate for 2013 was 12.4, a still lower value.)

This rate differs widely among ethnic groups. White women in the United States in 2010 had a birth rate of 12.5. By comparison, the birth rate for Asian women was 14.5, for African-American women, 15.1, 18.7 for Hispanic women, and 11.0 for American Indians and Alaska Natives.[9]

Ethnic Background. One of the most striking results of the 2010 census was the insight it provided on the increasing diversity of the American people. More than half of the growth in population in the United States between 2000 and 2010 was due to an increase in Hispanic population. That population grew from 35,305,818 in 2000 to 40,477,594 in 2010, an increase of 15,171,776, or 43 percent. The fraction of the US population made up of individuals from Hispanic or Latino backgrounds grew, therefore, from 12.5 percent in 2000 to 16.3 percent in 2010.[10]

An even larger increase in percentage of total US population was realized by individuals with an Asian background. In 2000, 10,242,998 Americans claimed an Asian background, compared to 14,674,252, an increase of 4,431,129, or 43.3 percent. Among the legal immigrants from Asia, the nationality that grew the fastest between 2000 and 2010 was Indians (an increase in population growth of 68 percent), followed by Filipinos (44 percent), Vietnamese (42 percent), Chinese (40 percent), and Koreans (39 percent).[11]

Urbanization. Another trend found in the 2010 census was the increasing urbanization of the United States. Following another long-term pattern, more and more people were moving out of rural and farm areas into urban areas. By 2010, 80.7 percent of all Americans lived in such areas. The growth rate in urban areas was 12.1 percent compared to a 9.7 percent growth rate in rural and farm areas. Seven of the most densely populated areas in the country are located in California, including the Los Angeles-Long Beach-Anaheim region, with nearly 7,000 people per square mile; the San Francisco-Oakland area, with 6,266 people per square mile; San Jose, with 5,820 people per square mile; and Delano, with 5,483 people per square mile.[12]

Overall, the 2010 U.S. census suggests that some major changes may be taking place in the nation's population structure. Numbers point to the growth of a larger, more urbanized, and more culturally diverse nation than has ever existed. How these changes may affect the social, political, economic, and moral fabric of American society is a question of increasing concern to many population experts.

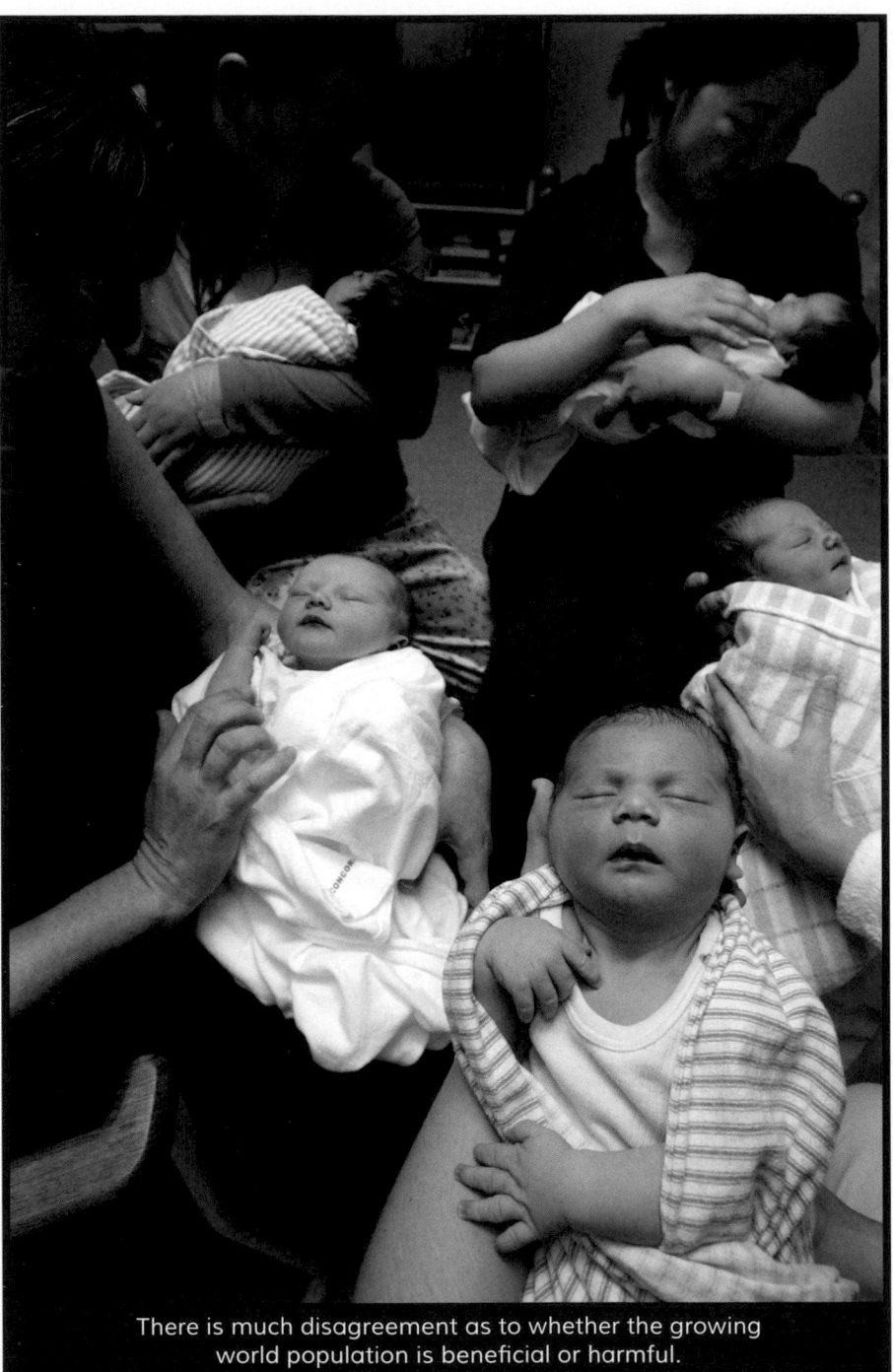

There is much disagreement as to whether the growing world population is beneficial or harmful. Here, new mothers hold their babies at a hospital in Australia.

CHAPTER 5

THE LIMITS TO GROWTH

"... THE CHIEF CAUSE FOR THE IMPENDING COLLAPSE of the world—the cause sufficient and by itself—is the enormous growth of the human population: the human flood. The worst enemy of life is too much life: the excess of human life."[1]

The idea contained in this statement summarizes the main point of this book: Overpopulation is a clear and present threat to the survival of the human race, and steps must be taken if human civilization is to survive into the future.

We should say at this point that not everyone agrees with that view. Some individuals in the United States and around the world believe that the dangers posed by overpopulation are exaggerated. They say that large populations can actually be good for a nation because they make more consumers available to purchase goods and help a nation's economy grow. Consider what David Osterfield, professor of political science, has to say about overpopulation:

> Contrary to the constant barrage of doomsday newspaper and television stories, the data clearly show that the

prospect of the Malthusian [overpopulation] nightmare is growing steadily more remote. The natural limits of what the earth can support are steadily receding, not advancing. Population growth is slowing while the supplies of food, resources, and even living space are increasing . . . In short, although there are now more people in the world than ever before, by any meaningful measure the world is actually becoming *relatively less population.*[2]

To gain a better idea about the concept of overpopulation and the risks it may pose to human civilization, let's look first at the concept of optimum population.

OVERPOPULATION VERSUS OPTIMUM POPULATION

No question is as fundamental to a discussion of population today than this one: Are there too many people in the world? Or, we may ask: Is the United States overpopulated? Is Canada? China? Nigeria?

Questions about population size are not unusual in biology. A wildlife expert might want to know, for example, if an island has become over-populated with deer. She can answer that question by measuring the resources—water, sunlight, food, and so on—available to deer on the island. Biologists use the term *carrying capacity* to describe the maximum number of animals that an environment can support. The carrying capacity of the island, for example, is the number of healthy deer that can live on the island.

The idea of carrying capacity can be applied to artificial environments, too. Farmers today often want to provide cows, sheep, chickens, and other animals with the minimum conditions necessary to keep the animals alive and healthy. So, biologists calculate the minimum amount of space, water, exercise, and other conditions an animal requires including the conditions available on the farm. Then they can tell the farmer the maximum number of animals his farm can support.

Perhaps you can imagine making this kind of biological calculation for humans. You could try to measure all the natural resources available on the Earth, and try to imagine every way possible to squeeze people together. Then you could calculate the number of people who could survive on Earth using all the resources and technology known.

Many scientists have tried to make such a calculation. They differ dramatically with the numbers they come up with, ranging from a low of fewer than two billion people to a high of about 1,000 billion people. In one review of sixty-five estimates that have been made to Earth's human carrying capacity, the most common guess was eight billion people, which, you'll notice, is not so very far away![3]

Most experts point out that the number one chooses for carrying capacity is not nearly as important as the conditions that will accompany that number. Can you imagine a planet with more than 1,000 billion people on it? Under such circumstances, human life would be similar to the life of a calf on some modem farms. Everyone would be restricted to his or her own "pen" of a few square meters in size. Very few people would be happy with this arrangement. Not many can even imagine that the techniques biologists use with farm animals could be applied to human populations either.

Instead, most of us understand that humans want more than the deer on an island or the calves on a farm are allowed for their survival. Humans also need jobs, travel, good health, the arts, education, interactions with other people, and all those other factors that make up human culture. Author Garrett Hardin has suggested that people interested in population issues think in terms of cultural carrying capacity.[4] That term refers not just to the number of people that can *survive* in an environment, but the number that can live a reasonably satisfactory lifestyle.

The problem is that people don't necessarily agree as to what is a "reasonably satisfactory lifestyle." Ask a resident of Botswana and a resident of Sweden that question. You are likely to get two very different answers. So population experts who try to measure cultural carrying capacity also get very different answers.

For example, Hardin estimated that the earth could support 300 billion people (about forty times its present size), if everyone lived like the average Ethiopian.[5] Another expert thinks that world population could

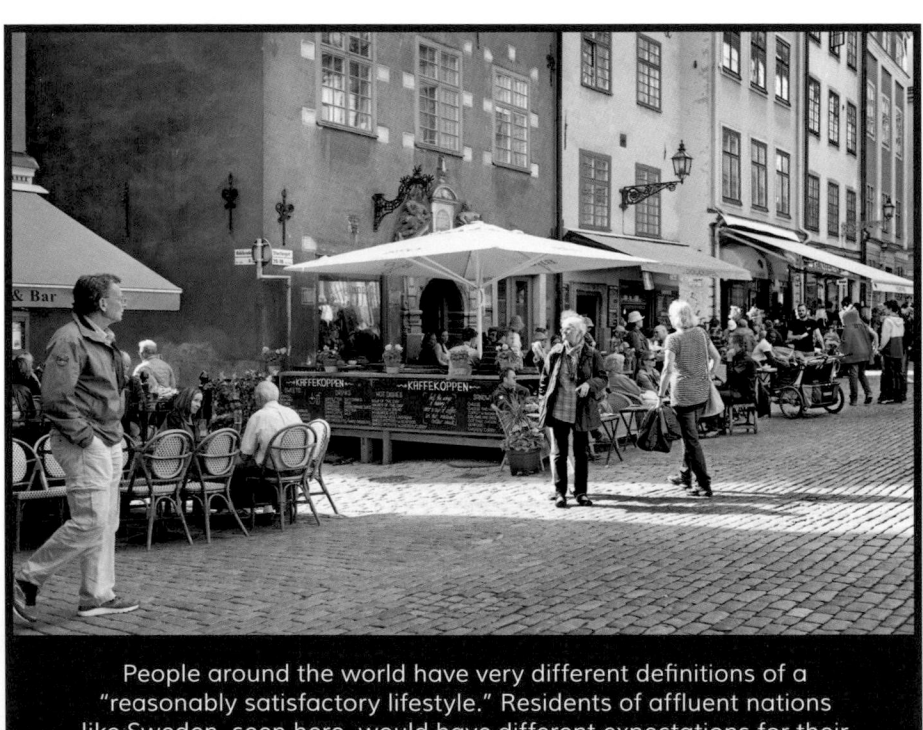

People around the world have very different definitions of a "reasonably satisfactory lifestyle." Residents of affluent nations like Sweden, seen here, would have different expectations for their standard of living as compared to a poor country like Ethiopia.

reach 59 billion (eight times its present size) if we would all adopt a life-style like that of the modern Chinese.[6] By either of those standards, the world is certainly not overpopulated today.

But most people would probably not choose to live at the poverty level, to just survive. Most people want enough food to eat, living space of their own, adequate fuel for cooking and heating, reasonable clothing, and the like. What kind of population could the earth sustain given *that* criterion?

In trying to answer that question, population experts use the concept known as optimum population. The optimum population of an area (a city, state, nation, or the world) is the largest population with a reasonably satisfactory lifestyle the area can sustain. Thus, optimum population is very similar to cultural carrying capacity. If the population of the area exceeds the optimum population, we can say the area is overpopulated.

Defining these terms still does not help much, however. The Earth's population today is just over seven billion. Some people think that number is too large and that the world is overpopulated. Other people think that seven billion may be just about right for a world population. Anything larger would result in overpopulation. Still others think the world's optimum population is much greater than seven billion, perhaps ten or fifteen billion. These people think that we are many years from reaching an optimum population for the Earth.

We are no closer to answering the most basic question: Is the world overpopulated? And which nations, if any, are overpopulated? Perhaps the question that we should focus on is what happens when a region, a nation, or the world becomes overpopulated? What kinds of changes can we expect to see and how happy will we be with those changes?

BACK TO THE BEGINNINGS: THE THEORIES OF THOMAS ROBERT MALTHUS

The debate about what constitutes optimum population goes back at least to the late eighteenth century. Probably the most famous name involved in this debate is Thomas Robert Malthus, an Englishman. Malthus was ordained as a clergyman at the age of twenty-two, although he soon became interested in economics. In 1804 he was appointed professor of history and political economy at the East India College in Haileyburg. He remained in that post until he died in 1834.[7]

The work for which Malthus is best remembered today, "An Essay on the Principle of Population," was first printed in 1798. The essay was rewritten and expanded seven times, with the last version published in 1872, thirty-eight years after Malthus's death. Because the seven editions of the essay differed considerably from each other, people often disagree as to what Malthus *really* had to say about population.

Malthus wrote his first "Essay" in response to a popular political notion of the time, namely that the future of the human race was bright and promising. Many scholars (including Malthus's father, Daniel) thought that the French and American revolutions had marked the dawn of a new age. They felt that humans were approaching an era of perfection in which poverty would be eliminated, disease would be conquered, wars would cease, and all human needs would be met.

Malthus held quite a different opinion. He believed that human progress was limited by certain natural factors, the most important being food. Specifically, he argued that population growth in a country would always occur more rapidly than would the supply of food.

Thomas Robert Malthus, economist and philosopher, believed there would be dire consequences for the world's increasing population.

Malthus said that population growth occurred geometrically, while the growth in food supplies grew only arithmetically. An example of a geometric series is one that doubles after a certain number of years. The series 1, 2, 4, 8, 16, 32, 64, and so on, is a geometric series. Malthus used as his example the country of Ireland, whose population at the time was seven million. Malthus predicted that in twenty-five years, Ireland's population would double to fourteen million. In the next generation, the population would double again, to twenty-eight million. Twenty-five years later the population would increase to fifty-six million . . . and so on.

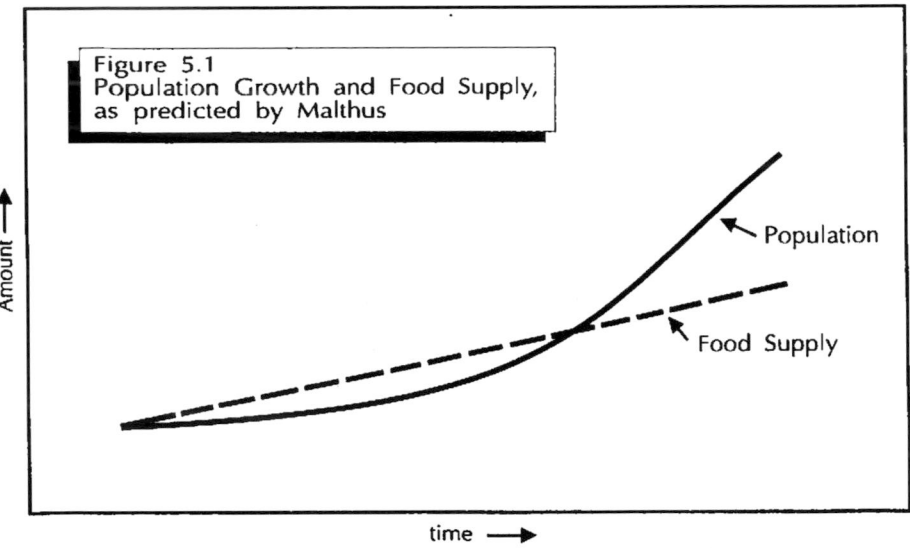

Figure 5.1
Population Growth and Food Supply, as predicted by Malthus

The solid line in Figure 5.1 shows the population growth that Malthus predicted for Ireland. He believed that this kind of growth was natural for all human societies. But, Malthus argued, the food supply cannot keep up with this rate of increase. The growth in food production can only occur arithmetically, he thought. An arithmetic series is one that increases by the same amount in each time period, for example the series 1, 2, 3, 4, 5 . . . The chart below compares an arithmetic increase and a geometric increase.

Time Period	1	2	3	4	5	6
Food Production (Arithmetic Growth)	1	2	3	4	5	6
Population Growth (Geometric Growth)	1	2	4	8	16	32

Assume, Malthus said, that farms in Ireland now produce just enough to feed its seven million people. Perhaps the food supply could double—as, for example, by improvements in farming methods—in the next twenty-five years, making it possible to feed the fourteen million population in that generation.

But could they continue to double their food output *every* twenty-five years? Malthus thought such a notion absurd. "In a few centuries," he said, "it would make every acre of land in the Island like a garden."[8] As a result, Malthus predicted that food supplies would only increase at the rate shown by the dotted line in Figure 5.1.

Based on this reasoning, Malthus drew what he thought was an inescapable conclusion: Under normal circumstances, population will continue to grow until it exceeds the food supply. At this point, people would begin to go hungry and starvation would become widespread. Epidemics would sweep across the land, and death rates would skyrocket. Eventually, the population would fall to a point where enough food would be available to feed everyone. Then, the whole process of population growth would begin again, only to be ended a few generations later with another round of starvation, disease, and warfare. The perfect human societies that his father and others predicted were impossible. Instead, population growth would forever lead to poverty, disease, and human misery.

Homeless people are served lunch at a soup kitchen. Malthus believed that helping the poor was not beneficial; in fact, he said it would only keep them alive so that they could reproduce and create future generations of poor people.

Malthus saw almost no way out of the limits placed by nature. Even the progress that seemed to be taking place around him was an illusion, he thought. For example, cowpox vaccinations seemed to be a way of reducing deaths from smallpox. But, Malthus argued, even if smallpox were conquered, some other disease would take its place.

He was convinced that human efforts to deal with problems were often misguided. The Poor Laws, for example, were intended to relieve the misery of England's most unfortunate. But that was not how they worked, Malthus said. Giving aid to the poor simply kept them alive and reproducing. The laws merely guaranteed that another poor and miserable generation would soon need assistance.

Similar arguments can be heard today about modern welfare systems. We should not try too hard to support the poor, some people believe. All we do is develop a permanent welfare class. Poverty and high reproduction rates are simply passed down, then, from generation to generation. As one political commentator wrote in 2011:

> The impact of food stamps, Section 8 housing subsidies, Medicaid, and other support programs has been to create a permanent welfare class which, in terms of skills and attitudes, is poorly equipped to return to work.[9]

TAKE ACTION!

You have been asked to serve as a population advisor to the island-state of Kibo. One of your first assignments is to analyze those factors that act as limits to population growth in the nation. Make a list of those factors, being as specific as possible. You might include, for example, food supplies, energy resources, and medical services. Arrange these factors in rank order, with the ones that are likely to be most important to the control of population growth in Kibo. When you have completed your list, think of at least one way in which the Kiboans can deal with each of these factors (such as filling in the bay to produce more arable land or limiting parents to one child each).

When you have finished this assignment for Kibo, repeat the exercise for the region (county, state, nation, etc.) in which you live. What changes can the people in your region reasonably expect to be able to make to reduce forthcoming problems of overpopulation?

Write a short essay summarizing what *you* have learned about the limits to growth in the modern world. Post your essay on a social media website and invite comments on your thoughts.

In later editions of the "Essay," Malthus acknowledged that this pattern could be altered. Unlike animals, humans can make conscious decisions that affect the rate of population growth. For example, delaying the age of marriage and avoiding sexual intercourse is likely to reduce the birth rate. And a lower birth rate tends to slow the rate of population growth.

Other kinds of behavior, like homosexuality and the use of birth control, also tend to reduce population growth. Of all these behaviors, Malthus considered only two (late marriage and sexual abstinence) to be morally acceptable options. Throughout his life, he opposed birth control as a means of limiting population.

MALTHUSIANS AFTER MALTHUS

Malthus had a profound influence on population experts in the decades after his death. The logic of his arguments seemed obvious. Population growth might continue for a while, but, after all, natural resources *are* limited. The time must come, therefore, when the famine, epidemic, warfare, and general misery that Malthus predicted would all occur.

The problem was that the real world seemed to contradict Malthus's vision. At certain times and in certain places, his predictions did come true, one example from Malthus's native country being the terrible potato famines in Ireland in the 1840s. But overall, these disasters were uncommon. Instead, humans around the world were healthier, better fed, living longer, and generally experiencing a better quality of life with each new generation. All this at the same time that population continued to increase. The reality of population growth and an improved standard of living raised doubts about Malthus's predictions.

Thus, population growth was simply a non-issue for most nations until well into the twentieth century. Malthus did continue to hold interest for population scholars and some public officials, but his ideas just seemed irrelevant to the real world. Scientists had apparently found ways to overcome the natural limits that had troubled Malthus. Perhaps technology could continue to hold off Malthusian disasters indefinitely.

Many decision-makers in the mid-twentieth century would probably have agreed with Sir John Boyd Orr's comment to the International Congress on Population and World Resources in Relation to the Family in 1948, when he said, ". . . if modern science is applied and Governments are willing to do it, we can feed and clothe and house as large a population as is likely to come in the next fifty or hundred years . . ."[10]

But a dramatic shift in the way people and governments viewed population growth began in the 1960s. Within one decade, the issue of population growth changed from being a non-issue to one of the world's great social problems. That shift is reflected in the views of two presidents of the United States. When asked as to whether he thought the government should be involved in birth control programs in 1959, President Dwight D. Eisenhower replied that he could not imagine "anything more emphatically that is not a proper political government activity or function or responsibility."[11] Only fifteen years later, President Richard Nixon (Eisenhower's former vice president) announced, "This [population] growth will produce serious challenge for our society. I believe that many of our present social problems may be related to [population growth]."[12]

President Nixon's comments came in the midst of a widespread revival of warnings about Malthusian disasters. The Irish economist's predictions were finally about to occur, according to many writers. Fears of population

President Nixon was the first modern US president to publicly acknowledge that overpopulation was a serious issue facing the country and the world.

catastrophes spawned a barrage of books, articles, speeches, organizations, and special events trumpeting the dangers of overpopulation.

Pessimism about population was the order of the day. Population experts were beginning to talk about applying triage to the nations of the world. *Triage* is a medical term for a procedure used when working with those wounded in battle or injured in disasters. Medical workers make decisions about the sequence in which the wounded are to be treated: Those who have the best chance of survival are treated first. The others are "set aside," as it were, and treated last, if they are still alive.

Similarly, in the 1960s and 1970s, some writers were making triage lists of nations. They were trying to decide which nations had population problems that were "treatable." Those nations should qualify for aid from wealthy countries. Other nations with "hopeless" population problems would have to be ignored. Their condition was so desperate, these experts said, that they were simply to be "let go." In their book *Famine—1975!*, for example, William and Paul Paddock decided that Haiti, Egypt, and India belonged in the "can't be-saved" group. The population situation in these nations was so bad, the authors wrote, that the United States should not bother to send them food. Tunisia and Pakistan, on the other hand, could still be saved, and American food should be sent to those nations.[13]

Very soon, the campaign against population growth became a tidal wave. Many thoughtful people had become convinced that most of the world's most serious problems were a result of out-of-control population growth.

At the World Population Conference in Bucharest, Romania, in 1974, the United States and other MDCs argued vigorously for controls on population growth, especially in the LDCs. They insisted that population growth was nullifying efforts to improve standards of living in the developing nations of the world. Economic aid was being wasted, they believed, on LDCs where populations were growing faster than were their economies.

TRIAGE FOR POPULATION PROBLEMS

You have learned about the concept of triage in relation to population control. Do you agree that decision-makers should attempt to choose countries to which assistance should be given to help them deal with their population problems? Look at a world map that shows birth rates in various countries around the world. One such map can be found on the World Bank website at http://data .worldbank.org/indicator/SP.DYN.CBRT.IN/countries?display=map. Decide which nations in the world are most worthy of receiving assistance with their population problems and make a triage list with those most in need at the top and those least in need at the bottom. Are there some nations you would leave off the list? Why or why not?

Support began to develop for the idea that only by reducing population growth could LDCs ever achieve economic development. Thus, adopting the principle of triage, the United States and other MDCs decided that foreign aid should be funneled to those nations with a commitment to population planning programs.

One feature of these programs, some experts thought, might be a more forceful approach to population control. Up to this time, most governments and private agencies had tried education and voluntary programs of population control. If we can only warn people about the dangers of overpopulation, they believed, they will see the need to limit family size.

But education and voluntary programs did not work very well. Populations around the world were still climbing in the 1960s and 1970s. Perhaps the time had come, some thought, to use force: coercive and involuntary approaches to population control. One of the most outspoken advocates of this approach was Paul Ehrlich, author of *The Population Bomb,* who stated, "We must have population control at home, hopefully through a system of incentives and penalties, but by compulsion if voluntary methods fail."[14] And Garrett Hardin wrote, "Coercion is a dirty word to most liberals now, but it need not forever be so . . . Freedom to breed will bring ruin to us all."[15]

Perhaps the most interesting point about the Bucharest conference was that most LDCs did not share this view of population growth. For

Paul Ehrlich, author of *The Population Bomb,* argued for government intervention to control population growth.

most of them, people were a valuable asset. The larger its population, the more potential a nation had, they believed. In fact, population growth often seemed to be a critical step in achieving economic development.

The LDCs resented the MDCs telling them to limit their populations. Population control sounded to the LDCs like a new form of colonialism. If the MDCs really cared, the LDCs said, they would provide *more* economic aid, not less. Only with improving economies could they hope to move through the demographic transition and achieve a high level of development themselves.

By the end of the 1970s, then, the United States and other MDCs had adopted a Malthusian view of population growth. That view was largely directed at the LDCs, however. The United States and various international agencies began to develop programs to help LDCs limit their population growth. At home, however, the United States government never developed an official population policy for its own people. And there was much less enthusiasm for such programs in the LDCs than in the MDCs.

WHAT ARE THE LIMITS TO GROWTH?

The basic assumption behind Malthusian theories is that Earth is a closed system; in other words, it contains only a set amount of certain natural resources. Our planet holds about 332.5 million cubic miles of water, and no more.[16] About 5,000,000,000,000,000,000,000 Btu (British thermal units) of sunlight strike Earth each day, and no more. And about a half trillion barrels of oil (by one estimate) are buried within Earth, and no more.[17] We can use all of a resource we want to, but only up to a set limit, the maximum amount of the resource that exists on the planet.

Malthus thought of Ireland (as well as the rest of the world) as a closed system. After all, he argued, Ireland had only a set amount of arable land (land that can be farmed). A farmer can grow only so much food on an acre of land. Thus the amount of food available to feed people is, in the long term, set.

One interesting point is that Malthus never recognized that he was living through a revolution—the Industrial Revolution. Limits that existed during his lifetime—the amount of work a single person could do, for example—would be far surpassed by the time he died. He could probably never have imagined that chemical fertilizers yet to be developed would double or triple the amount of a crop produced on an acre of land.

Malthusians today recognize this flaw in the "Essay." But they argue that the basic idea of the earth as a closed system is correct. No matter

Malthus believed that we have a limited food supply on earth and worried that eventually that supply would run out.

how clever we become with our technology, we do have to accept the limitations of natural resources, they say. And by the 1960s, some experts were trying to find out exactly what those limitations were.

One of the more interesting studies was begun in April of 1968. A group of thirty individuals from ten nations met to discuss world problems. It was later expanded to seventy people from twenty-five nations and became the Club of Rome. The Club initiated a study of the way five major systems interacted within these world problems. One of the five systems was population growth.

The final report of this study was in the form of a book entitled *The Limits to Growth*. The book echoed some familiar Malthusian themes. It argued that natural resources place a limit on population growth, industrial development, and control of pollution. Since Malthus's time, the book argued, the world may have been lulled into a sense of false security. The food supply had kept pace with population growth between 1800 and 1950. Malthus appeared to be wrong.

But the rapid growth of food supplies came at a high cost. Fertilizers, mechanized farming, pesticides, and other modern agricultural techniques required large amounts of energy. Huge quantities of coal, oil, and natural gas were used up in order to increase the food supply. Perhaps the food problem was solved (for now), but now we were in danger of running out of energy. Malthus was not wrong, they concluded. His predicted future had just been delayed a few generations.

In a major conclusion, the authors of *Limits* wrote:

> Given the finite and diminishing stock of nonrenewable resources and the finite space of our globe, the principle must be generally accepted that growing numbers of people will eventually imply a lower standard of living . . .[18]

This point of the book was entirely in keeping with general ideas about population growth at the time. A growing population was placing unacceptable demands on limited resources. As population continued to grow, these resources would begin to disappear. Those resources that were available would be spread more thinly among a larger population. Population growth, therefore, can only lead to a poorer standard of living for people throughout the world.

The theme of *Limits* also appeared in the work of economist Kenneth Boulding. Writing in the 1970s, Boulding claimed that the world had long been pursuing a "cowboy economics." By that he meant that people and nations were acting as if they lived on an endless frontier with unlimited resources. Especially in the United States and other MDCs, a new frontier was "just over the hill." When the United States ran out of oil, for example, it would simply start to import oil from other nations. When Canada ran out of farmland, it could make more by filling wetlands. There was always "more" somewhere that could be found and developed.

But, Boulding pointed out, it was time to think of the world in a new and more realistic way. Instead of an endless frontier, we needed to think of Earth as a spacecraft. All the resources we would ever have were closed up inside our Spaceship Earth. When we used up those resources, they were gone forever. Importing oil and filling wetlands did not change this fact. All natural resources are, ultimately, limited.

The significance of this concept to population growth is obvious. We could continue to add passengers to our Spaceship Earth, Boulding said. But in doing so, we would only be making life more and more difficult for everyone inside. Unrestrained population growth could ultimately only lead, he believed, to a poorer life for all humans.

The warnings about population growth from Malthus, Ehrlich, Hardin, Boulding, and other Malthusians have made their impact on public opinion. Many population experts, government officials, and ordinary citizens accept as fact that overpopulation is a serious and worldwide problem. Almost any newspaper or magazine you read today continues to warn of the human misery that results from population growth.

But this viewpoint is only one side of the story. Other population experts, government officials, and ordinary citizens take quite a different view of population growth. To these observers, larger populations do not necessarily create social problems. In fact, population growth may even be desirable. In the next chapter, we will examine this view of population growth.

CHAPTER 6
THE MYTH OF OVERPOPULATION?

MALTHUS'S THEORY OF POPULATION HAD ITS CRITICS as soon as it appeared in print. One writer, Thomas Doubleday, argued in 1842 that Malthus's ideas were too simple. He reminded Malthus of a well-known and intriguing fact about population growth: As a person's standard of living improves, she or he is inclined to have fewer children. Even in Malthus's time, people realized that the rich tend to have few babies and the poor many. In that case, Doubleday wrote, the best way to control population growth is by making life better for everyone. As a nation's standard of living improves, he said, its birth rate will fall, and population problems will disappear.[1]

ANTI-MALTHUSIANS IN THE 1980S

The United Nations (UN) sponsors a World Population Conference every ten years. Between the 1974 meeting in Bucharest (discussed in Chapter 5) and the 1984 meeting in Mexico City, some remarkable changes in world

A crowded street in Shanghai. The Chinese city is the most populated in the world, with about twenty-four million people in 2013.

opinions about population growth occurred. At the earlier conference, the United States and most MDCs had been leaders in the campaign for population control, but most LDCs had been suspicious of and resistant to this movement.

Ten years later, in 1984, most LDCs as well as most MDCs were enthusiastic supporters of the concept of population control. The vast majority of the world's nations were committed to programs of one kind or another that would reduce birth rates. Only one major nation at Mexico City argued against population control: the United States.

The US delegation argued that the notion of a "global population problem" was a myth. If anything, the United States claimed, the actions of governments around the world in the preceding decade had worsened problems by interfering with people's efforts to improve themselves economically. The only action that was needed, the US delegates said, was to let free-market economics work. In that way, nations would prosper, the demographic transition would take place, and population "problems" would disappear.[2]

What happened between 1974 and 1984 to reverse the US position on population? In terms of population trends, not very much happened. Most MDCs continued to experience declining birth rates. Most LDCs continued to experience high (if slowly declining) birth rates. Population still raged "out of control" (according to Malthusians) across the greatest part of the planet. And supposedly population-related problems such as pollution and depletion of natural resources continued everywhere.

The one factor that *had* changed during this time was the political climate in the United States. In 1980, the American people elected a new president, Ronald Reagan, with a conservative political philosophy. With

Reagan in the White House, population authorities who had been largely ignored for many years were now in positions of influence. For the first time in decades, a non-Malthusian view of population issues was being heard in government circles.[3]

THE ViEWS OF JULIAN SIMON

Perhaps the best known spokesperson for this view was Julian L. Simon. Simon, a professor of economics, authored a number of important articles and books on population, including *The Ultimate Resource* (1981) and, along with Herman Kahn, *The Resourceful Earth* (1984).

Simon argued, first of all, that the Malthusian doomsayers of the 1960s and 1970s were simply wrong. The catastrophes those writers predicted just did not come to pass. Instead, Simon claimed, the amount of food available per person worldwide had increased since 1945; land, natural resources, and energy were not in short supply; pollution had not increased as a result of population growth; and the standard of living worldwide was better in the long run than it had been four decades ago. Furthermore, Simon suggested, predictions of increasing population growth in the future were likely to be wrong. In other words, the fundamental arguments put forth by the Malthusians were wrong.[4]

How can incorrect ideas about population growth have become so popular and so widely accepted? Simon asked. The answer, he suggested, is that alarmists of the 1960s and 1970s used "bad information, phony arguments, fears of taxation, fears of communism, self-interest, racism," and dozens of other techniques for selling the myth of overpopulation. The result of this campaign, according to Simon, was that "tens of millions of US taxpayers' money is being used to tell the governments and people of other countries that they ought to take strong measures to control their fertility" and to tell those in the United States that "fewer Americans should be born."[5]

But Simon was more than a critic of modern Malthusians. He also proposed a theory as to why population growth is good. In general, his ideas bear some resemblance to those of Karl Marx, the founder of Communism and an anti-Malthusian, although they are far more carefully developed.

Simon believed, for example, that a large population creates a large demand for goods and services. Think what would happen, as an example, if the United States had twice the population in 2050 that it has today. The demand for televisions, cars, homes, recreational vehicles, clothes, roads, airports, schools, and other products and services would be at least twice as great as it is today. What a spur to the economy that would be!

Further, with twice the population, there would be twice as many workers to meet all this new demand. More workers in many new plants would be turning out new products for the growing population. More teachers, engineers, doctors, waiters, and computer personnel would be needed to meet the growing demand for services. Overall, an increased population would be an enormous incentive for economic growth.

Simon did recognizes two potential problems with this model, however. First, one has to compare the long-term vs. short-term effects of population growth. To begin with, no one can argue about the economic costs of an additional child. The child is dependent on its parents for food, housing, clothing, education, health care, and all its other needs. In that sense, the child is clearly a drain on its parents' resources. And, in a

Author and economist Julian Simon saw the increasing population as positive for the economy and believed that the greater the population, the greater the demand for goods.

broader sense, the births of many children constitutes a high immediate cost to a nation's economy.

But these costs are short-term costs, Simon argued. One must also think about the contributions that child and those children will make in the long run. Someday they will be workers, inventors, artists, taxpayers, productive members of the community. He wrote:

> An additional child is, from the economic point of view, like a laying chicken, a cacao tree, a new factory, or a new house. A baby is a durable good in which someone must invest heavily long before the grown adult begins to provide returns on the investment.[6]

The Malthusian response to this position raises a second possible objection to Simon's theory. That objection is that children are unlikely to be a greater economic benefit than economic handicap, because they use up a nation's limited resources. As population grows, fewer of those resources are available to each person in the society. Thus, the quality of life in the society diminishes, as Malthus predicted.

Simon's answer to this argument is that natural resources are *not* limited. In fact, for all practical purposes, the earth's resources—land, food, energy, minerals, and so on—are infinite. As an example, people worry about running out of arable land. But when that threat does occur, humans become creative. They fill wetlands, irrigate deserts, build dikes, and in other ways expand the actual supply of land.

One can argue, in theory, that natural resources are limited. But in actual fact, humans throughout history have always found ways to expand those limits. Thus, the notion that the natural supply of resources limits population growth—Malthus's original concept—is wrong.

Simon argued that even the Club of Rome had come to accept this fact. Only four years after *The Limits to Growth* first appeared, the Club reversed its views on population growth. By 1976 it was arguing for *increased* growth. In fact, some observers believe that the Club's original report actually misrepresented the potential effects of growth.[7] Simon goes so far as to call the report's original conclusions "lies."

Simon did admit that temporary shortages of natural resources may sometimes occur. A nation may, indeed, seem to run out of some raw material that its industries need. But we should not be concerned about such problems. He reminded us that "Necessity is the mother of invention." We should, in fact:

> welcome the scarcity problems that are caused by increasing population and rising incomes, because if problems do not arise, solutions will not be evoked. And the entire process of scarcity problems arising and then getting solved almost always leaves us better off than if the problems had never arisen.[8]

Solving such problems is certainly possible, Simon went on to say, because a greater population surely has a large number of geniuses who could come up with solutions for those problems. A growing population contains, therefore, not only the potential for new problems, but also the human resources needed to solve those problems.

Finally, Simon argued strongly against coercive population control programs. Such programs require people to have fewer children than they might *want* to have. He recalled that some writers in the 1960s and 1970s called for strong controls on population. American sociologist and demographer Kingsley Davis remarked in 1974, for example, that "over-reproduction—that is, the bearing of more than 2 children—is a worse crime than most and should be outlawed."[9] Simon's position was

Julian Simon supported the individual's right to choose family size and was opposed to any government intervention on this issue.

just the opposite. He thought that "it is good for people to be able, as much as possible, to decide how to run their own lives . . . I am unqualifiedly in favor of all these policies to increase the individual's ability to achieve the family size she or he chooses."[10]

ARE MDCS UNDERPOPULATED?

In 1967 Kingsley Davis published an important essay in the journal *Science.* In this essay, Davis discussed current efforts to bring population growth under control. He described the attempts that would be needed to halt population growth entirely, that is, to reach zero population growth (ZPG), that point at which the number of births is equal to the number of deaths. The population is then stabilized; it neither grows nor shrinks.

Davis felt that voluntary efforts to reach a ZPG goal were unlikely to succeed. Public and private agencies would have to work much more aggressively to control the birth rate efficiently enough to reach population stability.

Davis's article inspired an active debate over birth control policy. It also stimulated a new population movement organized around the concept of ZPG. Since 1969, the leading organization for that movement has been Population Connection, a private, nonprofit organization, originally known as Zero Population Growth, Inc., that seeks to achieve zero population growth throughout the world.

Many observers in the late 1960s thought that ZPG probably could not be realized without strong, coercive action by governments. Those same observers in the late 1980s began to see a world in which ZPG is not only possible, but highly likely. Birth rates in most MDCs have fallen well below replacement level. Replacement level is the number of children that women in a country must bear, on the average, to maintain a constant population.

In theory, the replacement level should be 2.0; in other words, each woman would have 2.0 children. The father and mother would be exactly replaced by their two offspring in the next generation. The country's population would neither increase nor decrease.

In reality, the replacement level is slightly greater than 2.0 in all societies. Children who die young, for example, never grow old enough to have children of their own. Thus the replacement level must be greater than 2.0. In the United States in the second decade of the twenty-first century, the replacement level was 2.1, and in countries with high infant death rates, the replacement level may have to be as high as 2.5.

In most MDCs today, women are having, on the average, far fewer than 2.1 children. The rate in most European Union countries is currently less than 2.0. It is lowest in Portugal (1.21), Spain (1.27), and Poland (1.29), and highest in France (1.99), Ireland (1.96), and Iceland (1.93). Overall, the average fertility rate for the European Union in 2014 was 1.55.[11] At the same point in time, the fertility rate in the United States was 1.9 and in Canada, 1.6.[12] These figures mean that in all of these nations, women were not producing enough children to maintain the nation's population at its current size.

The effect on population size of falling birth rates does not show up in a nation for many years. Based on birth rates in 2013, for example, the population of the United States will continue to increase until about the year 2100, at which time the nation should reach zero population growth.[13]

This effect, in fact, has already occurred in some Western European nations. In Germany, for example, the birth rate has been below replacement level for some time. Between 1980 and 1985, that nation's German-born population began to decline for the first time in more than three hundred years. The total population would have begun to decline, except for the fact that immigration into the country has actually increased Germany's population. By 1985 Belgium and Hungary had also reached zero population growth, and their populations are also now declining.[14]

For a world concerned about overpopulation for the last few decades, these changes represent a surprising trend.

ARE WE EXPERIENCING A "BIRTH DEARTH"?

What is the significance of falling birth rates in MDCs? One book that has tried to answer that question is Ben Wattenberg's *The Birth Dearth*, published in 1987. Until his death in 2015, Wattenberg was a senior fellow at the American Enterprise Institute. He had thought and written about population issues for more than twenty-five years.

The title of his book refers to the decline in birth rates in the United States, Western Europe, Japan, and other MDCs. Wattenberg argued that falling birth rates represent a serious threat to those nations that make up what he calls "the modern, industrial, free world."[15] He pointed out that the fraction of people living in those nations dropped from 22% in 1950 to 15% in 1987 and will probably reach 9% by the year 2030.

This change presents a number of major problems for the free world, Wattenberg believed. First, as Julian Simon had argued, population decrease will result in fewer people to buy and make products, resulting in the weakening of economies. Second, as "free nations" lose population, they will have to reduce the size of their military forces, allowing the balance of power to shift to the "non-free nations" of the world. Wattenberg raised the threat of Tunisia or Iraq or some other nation becoming a powerful military force in the world.

Third, falling birth rates mean that the average age of populations in the "free nations" will continue to rise. A larger number of older people in the population means greater demand for medical care and lower productivity among workers, Wattenberg feared. Fourth, he worried about the personal unhappiness people are likely to feel as they grow older with fewer or no children as part of their lives. He thought that young women who have chosen a career over a family "will probably live to regret it."[16]

Finally, the most controversial part of Wattenberg's argument may have been his concern about the growth of minorities in "free nations," especially in the United States. He pointed out that birth rates among blacks, Hispanics, and other non-European immigrants remained high.

Ben Wattenberg argued that reducing populations would mean a weaker nation in the future.

That trend means that the fraction of "white European stock" in the United States was continually decreasing, from about 80% in 1987 to a projected 60% in 2080.

Wattenberg thought that this trend means that "what's coming down the road demographically is asking for extra trouble." He feared that a declining "white European stock" was likely to cause "resentment" and lead to "social turbulence."[17]

Echoes of Wattenberg's concerns could be heard in political debates in the early 1990s. As the nation's economy remained weak, politicians sometimes placed blame on "other groups" who had come to the United States and placed unfair stress on the nation's economy. For example, California's governor Pete Wilson said in 1991 that one reason for the state's enormous budget deficit was the growing population of Hispanics who placed huge burdens on the state's welfare system. Also, presidential candidate Pat Buchanan's "America First" campaign in the 1992 primaries sometimes carried overtones of Wattenberg's ideas. As the nation's economy continued to suffer, relations between members of the nation's "white European stock" and its newest citizens were often strained.

THE DEBATE CONTINUES

The debate with regard to overpopulation has now been raging for nearly half a century.

So who should we believe? Are Malthus, Ehrlich, Hardin, Boulding, and other "alarmists" correct? Is overpopulation the root cause for most of the world's social problems? Or should we listen to Simon and other anti-Malthusians? Is the world's population problem greatly overrated?

Most professional demographers probably belong in neither of these extreme camps. The most common position seems to be somewhere between the "population growth must end" and "population growth is not so bad" camps.

CHAPTER 7

THE CONSEQUENCES OF OVERPOPULATION

THE POPULATION THEORY PRESENTED BY MALTHUS in the early 1800s has one serious problem: In practice, it has been wrong far more often than it has been right. The theory has a strong appeal to the logical mind. But what happens when one looks at the real world?

POPULATION AND FOOD

The first observation one can make is that population usually does not grow geometrically, as Malthus had assumed. In some places and at some times it does, but not in most MDCs for the last few decades, for example. In fact, population has actually begun to decrease in some of those countries. The rate of population growth has also slowed in many LDCs.

Moreover, food resources are not necessarily produced arithmetically, as Malthus had also predicted. In fact, one of the remarkable facts about the last 150 years has been the ability of farmers to increase food production geometrically, at least in some places at some times.

A farmer harvests his wheat crop with the help of a grain auger. Food production has increased as new farming technology is developed.

Consider, for example, how agricultural practices have improved in the United States in the last two centuries. In 1866 American farmers produced about 170 million bushels of wheat, with a yield of about 11.0 bushels per acre. Over time, those numbers rose to 635 million bushels at 11.9 bushels per acres fifty years later, 1,315.60 million bushels (26.5 bushels per acre) in 1961, and 2,163.02 million bushels (46.1 bushels per acre) in 2011.[1] And this progress occurred while the number of farms, farmers, and land planted to crops decreased substantially over the decades.

Much of the world experienced similar agricultural success, especially in the last fifty years. Between 1950 and 1984, for example, the amount of grain harvested worldwide increased from 631 million tons to 1.65 billion tons. That represents a gain of 2.6 times at a time when the world population increased by only 1.9 times.[2] During the same period, the average number of calories available per day to people around the world increased from 2,340 to 2,630.[3]

Population expert Julian Simon reviewed the evidence for increased food production and concluded: "Most agricultural economists agree that the trend has been toward improvement in the food supply of almost every main segment of the world's population."[4]

The world's farmers, then, have been remarkably successful in increasing the amount of food produced per capita between the time of Malthus and the present day. How was this accomplished? The answer can be expressed in one word: technology.

During Malthus's time, that technology was farm machinery. The Industrial Revolution made possible tractors, combines, cultivators, and other kinds of mechanical devices that vastly increased the amount of work a single person could do.

In more recent years, technology has produced a broader variety of techniques: new kinds of seed, chemical fertilizers, pesticides, and even more sophisticated machinery. The use of this technology has made possible the rapid expansion of agriculture in the United States and other MDCs after 1950. By the mid-1960s, that technology was also being exported to LDCs. The dramatic changes that took place in those LDCs as a result is known as the Green Revolution.

REVOLUTIONIZING AGRICULTURE

During the 1960s, agricultural scientists searched for ways to improve the productivity of farmers in LDCs. One approach was to invent new plant varieties that would do well in certain places. For example, dwarf varieties of rice and wheat especially suited to tropical climates were bred. The yield from these varieties was 200 to 300% over traditional varieties.[5]

The structure of the new plants also allowed for increased use of chemical fertilizers. The introduction of new wheat and rice varieties in India, for example, resulted in a tenfold increase in the use of chemical fertilizers between 1965 and 1975. As a result of this kind of technology, India became self-sufficient in grain production by the mid-1970s. The nation even began to worry about finding ways to store its surplus crops.[6]

The Green Revolution also involved the transfer of agricultural techniques that had worked well in the MDCs to LDCs. Modern methods of irrigation, use of pesticides, and mechanized equipment are examples. The use of pesticides by farmers in LDCs, for example, increased by an average of 7 to 8 percent every year between 1970 and 1990.[7]

To many observers, the accomplishments of the Green Revolution were almost miraculous. The wheat harvest in India tripled between 1965 and 1983. During the same period, Indonesia doubled its production of rice.[8] Overall, some authorities claim that 10 million hectares of cropland planted in new varieties now feed 500 million people in LDCs.[9]

THE PESSIMISTS' VIEW OF FOOD PRODUCTION IN THE 1990S

So were the world's farmers proving Malthus wrong? The data from the Green Revolution would seem to say so. Yet many population authorities—we'll call them the Pessimists—were not so sure. The explosion in food production following the Green Revolution, they predicted, was not likely to continue for long. In support, they pointed to some troubling statistics from the last half of the 1980s. For example, the production of grain worldwide began to slow in 1985 and 1986. Then, in 1987, 1988, and 1989, it began to decrease. In this three-year period, the world's people consumed more food than they produced.[10] During the last half of the 1980s, grain production leveled off in India, Indonesia, Mexico, and other nations where the Green Revolution had been most successful. By 1990 it began to look as if the miracle of the Green Revolution had become somewhat tarnished.

The Pessimists point to a number of factors that have contributed to this decline in agricultural output. First, some lands are now being overfarmed. During the peak of the Green Revolution, farmers began to make use of marginal lands which are highly susceptible to erosion. After a few productive years, valuable topsoil begins to wash away and crops can no longer be grown on the land.

By one estimate, eighty million hectares of cropland in India, sixty million hectares in one part of China, forty-seven million hectares in Ethiopia's central plateau, and about the same area in Madagascar had been seriously eroded. In the United States, more than 25% of the nation's croplands were being threatened by erosion under the existing level of farming.[11] In response to this threat, the US government withdrew 11% of the nation's farmland from use. Because this land had become too susceptible to erosion to continue farming, it was converted to grassland and woodland.[12]

Also, new farmlands placed heavy demand on water resources. In many areas of the world, water was being withdrawn from the ground faster than it could be replaced by natural processes. By some estimates, the water table was dropping six to forty-eight inches a year beneath a quarter of the irrigated cropland in the United States.[13] As water resources were being depleted in some of these areas, farming had to be cut back.

Soil erosion can be caused by overfarming or overgrazing. Much farmland has been lost due to erosion, and as a result there is less land for growing crops.

The Pessimists also pointed out the high energy costs of the Green Revolution. Most chemical fertilizers and pesticides are made from fossil fuels (coal, oil, and natural gas), which are also used in the operation of farm machinery. In the late 1960s, few people worried about our supplies of fossil fuels. By the early 1980s, many agricultural experts realized that fossil fuels were becoming more and more expensive as the supplies become less and less available. As that happened, Green Revolution technology also become more expensive and less suitable for LDCs.

Finally, people were becoming more conscious of the effect of Green Revolution technology on the environment. In the 1960s, farmers thought little about the effects of pesticides on the environment. Before long, more of them began to recognize the damage these chemicals can have on other forms of life. They also began to see how quickly pests can develop an immunity to pesticides.

Overall, these factors pointed out an important reality about the Green Revolution. Although that revolution certainly achieved remarkable results in the 1960s, 1970s, and early 1980s, the technology introduced by the Green Revolution carried with it some serious problems. We cannot expect the accomplishments of the first three decades to be continued through later generations.

THE PESSIMISTS' VIEW OF WORLDWIDE HUNGER

Another feature of the world's food situation troubles the Pessimists. One can talk about worldwide trends in food supplies. But emphasizing trends often hides important differences among regions of the world. For example, no one is likely to argue that the United States, Canada, and other MDCs suffer from food shortages. To be sure, hunger does exist in these countries, but its cause is not lack of food. After all, for many decades, the US government has been shipping surplus food to needy nations throughout the world. And it has been paying farmers not to grow crops for many years.

The situation among LDCs, however, is very different. In Africa, for example, per capita production of grain peaked in 1967. By the early 1990s, it had declined by 27%.[14] In 1986 the World Bank estimated the number of "food insecure" people in Africa to be one hundred million. The term *food insecure* is used for those who do not have enough food for normal health and physical activity.

In Ethiopia, Nigeria, and Zaire, the number of food insecure people was 14.7 million, 13.7 million, and 12 million, respectively. The most desperate nations were Chad, where 47% of the population was food insecure, followed by Somalia (42%), Mozambique (42%), and Uganda (40%).[15]

In the late twentieth century, a similar trend had begun in Latin America. In the 1930s, Latin America was exporting more grain than was North America. As recently as 1970, Latin American nations were still exporting food (four million tons) to other parts of the world. By 1981, however, per capita food production in Latin American nations had reached its peak. After that, per capita production began to fall at a rate of about by 7% per year. The United Nations World Food Council estimated in the late 1980s that the number of malnourished preschoolers in Peru, as one example, increased from 42% to 68% between 1980 and 1983. Based on its research, the Council expressed the view that "earlier progress in fighting hunger, malnutrition and poverty has come to a halt or is being reversed in many parts of the world."[16]

A decrease in food production presents a second, less obvious, problem for LDCs. Reduced production means, of course, that more people go hungry. But beyond that, it means that food has to be imported, and imported food costs money. Most of the countries that have to import food are very poor. Those same countries are likely to have very large debts to banks in the MDCs. They are thus caught in a difficult bind: Should they use their scarce finances to pay off their debts or to buy food for their people?

Mexico's debt to other nations in 1986 was equal to 80% of its gross national product (GNP). (GNP is a measure of the total value of goods and services in a nation.) Sudan and Zaire had debts of 110% and 189%, respectively. Thus, Zaire owed other countries nearly twice as much as the total value of all goods and services in its country! One wonders how nations can make much progress in solving their hunger problems with such massive foreign debts.[17]

AN OPTIMISTIC VIEW OF WORLDWIDE HUNGER

Is the world's hunger problem really this bad? Another group of population experts—we'll call them the Optimists—say no. They argue that the world's food supply is much better off than people realize.

The Optimists have a difficult case to make. Most of us are familiar with newspaper and television pictures of starving people in Africa. We have heard for years that millions of people are hungry and starving throughout the world. Could this view really be wrong?

The Optimists admit that hunger and starvation do exist. But they do not accept the picture painted by the Pessimists. They do not think that food supplies are a serious problem worldwide. Julian Simon once stated their case as follows:

> Contrary to popular impression, the per capita food situation has been improving for the three decades since World War II, the only decades for which we have acceptable data. We also know that famine has progressively diminished for at least the past century. And there is strong reason to believe that human nutrition will continue to improve into the indefinite future, even with continued population growth.[18]

The basis for Simon's beliefs, and those of other Optimists, is the idea that the earth's physical resources are not what they seem. We think that humans are limited by fixed amounts of land, water, metals, fossil fuels, and other natural resources. This may be true in theory; for example, no one can argue against the fact that the amount of water on the Earth is fixed.

But, the Optimists argue, those limitations have no meaning in real life. If we seem to be running out of a resource, the reason is social or political or economic. The world—including Africa and Latin America—does or can produce enough food to feed all its people. If hunger and starvation exist, the reason is not that enough food cannot be grown. It is that nations lack the will to produce, obtain, and distribute food.

A prominent member of the Optimist camp was David Hopper, who, until his death in 2011, was Senior Vice President for Policy, Planning, and Research at the World Bank. Hopper put the case this way:

> The world's food problem does not arise from any physical limitation on potential output or any danger of unduly stressing the environment. The limitations on abundance

A mother begs with her child in India. Some people blame politics and government for poverty rather than overpopulation.

are to be found in the social and political structures of nations and in the economic relations among them.[19]

Some Optimists have pointed out that the Pessimists raised alarms about food shortages in the 1960s and again in the 1970s. But in neither case did the terrible predictions come true. Newer alarms of the 1980s are unlikely to be correct either, say the Optimists.

First of all, they argue, the amount of arable land can still be increased. In the book *The Resourceful Earth*, economics professor D. Gale Johnson argues that there is a "substantial potential for expanding the amount of cultivable land in South America, Africa, and South-east Asia."[20] Simon agreed with that view. He believed that "the amount of agricultural land has been, and still is, increasing substantially, and it is likely to continue to increase where needed.[21]

Even more important, the Optimists say, is to make better use of the arable land now available. The most frequent recommendation is to increase the use of irrigation. Roger Revelle, former director of the Center for Population Studies at Harvard University, sees no reason why farmers in the LDCs could not achieve the same agricultural efficiency as American farmers. He pointed out that productivity in LDCs could be increased by a factor of 2, 3, 4, or more. In Bangladesh, for example, better use of irrigation and more efficient farming could increase yields from their level of 1.5 metric tons per hectare to the US average of 7.0 metric tons per hectare.[22]

The real problem behind food shortages, most Optimists agree, is one of economics, not natural resources. Governments in some LDCs simply do not place a high enough priority on raising food for their people. They set food prices at very low levels, too low for farmers to make much profit. The governments do this to keep the cost of living low for those who live in urban areas, among other reasons. Farmers are thus not encouraged to increase crop yields.

In the 1970s in India, the Philippines, Bangladesh, Pakistan, and Senegal, the price farmers got for rice was 30% less than the price on the world market. In Tanzania, the price was 70% less![23] The solution to food shortages in such cases, Johnson argued, is for those nations to change their economic policies. They need to raise the price paid for crops so that farmers will want to grow more.

The National Research Council's 1986 report on "Population Growth and Economic Development" took a position somewhere between that of the Optimists and Pessimists. It admitted that changes in governmental policies probably could increase food production in many nations. However, it also recognized that natural factors, such as the quality of soil, could impose a limit on the amount of progress that could be achieved.

One point of disagreement in the debate between Pessimists and Optimists is time. Did the changes in food production of the late 1980s represent a new trend? Was the world finally seeing the first signs of

A rice farmer in the Philippines plants in the mud of his field. Farmers in some countries, like the Philippines, still receive an unfair rate for their crops.

a Malthusian disaster? Or were these years "quirks"? Was production destined to rise again in the 1990s and into the twenty-first century? Will growth in agriculture once again catch up with population growth in LDCs, as it has so often in the past? At this point, no one can answer any of these questions with any certainty.

OTHER ISSUES RELATED TO POPULATION GROWTH

When you think of "population problems," you may first think of issues such as food shortages, hunger, and starvation, as described above. But growing populations produce other effects, too. They can have a dramatic impact on a host of other issues, such as the availability of natural resources like land, water, and mineral resources; quality of the natural environment; Earth's climate; and the quality of life.

How serious are these additional effects of population growth? As with food and hunger issues, Pessimists and Optimists differ about the answer to this question. Some experts believe that humans will eventually be able to solve all these problems in spite of increases in population. Others disagree strongly. They suggest that the very survival of human civilization depends on humans beginning to act aggressively to reduce population growth and, equally important, reducing the rate of consumption by people who already have more than they need to live safe, healthy, happy lives. One example of this belief is a warning made by John Guillebaud, emeritus professor of family planning and reproductive health at University College London in 2006. He cautioned, "Unless we reduce the human population humanely through family planning, nature will do it for us through violence, epidemics or starvation."[24]

WHAT IS THE STATUS OF NATURAL RESOURCES?

Population Pessimists warn that overpopulation must ultimately and inevitably cause the loss of a host of natural resources, ranging from water to land to forests to plant and animal life to fossil fuels and other sources of energy, all of which exist on Earth in limited amounts. Read what the Executive Director of the United Nations Population Fund had to say about this issue in 1988:

> In rural areas of developing countries, increasing numbers and concentrations of poor, mostly landless people are being forced to destroy their own resource base. In their search for food, water, fuel, and fodder, they use up wood faster than it is being grown, farm marginal land at non-sustainable levels, deplete water supplies and overgraze rangelands with increasing numbers of animals.[25]

This statement represents the Pessimists' view of the state of the world's natural resources of land, wood, wildlife, fossil fuels, metals, and other minerals. That view is essentially the same as that of food resources, namely, that some ultimate limit for each resource exists. As population grows, we use up more of that resource. Sooner or later, we run out of the resources.

The objective of the Club of Rome study was to estimate how soon those natural resources would be gone. *The Limits to Growth* predicted, for example, that Earth's supply of gold would be used up by 1983, its mercury resources by 1985, and its lead resources by 1998.[26] Similar projections were made for aluminum, chromium, coal, iron, natural gas, petroleum, and other resources.

Other experts pointed out errors in the reasoning used in making these predictions. They predicted that reserves of natural resources would probably last two, three, or more times longer than the estimates made in *Limits*.[27] Yet, most Pessimists continue to agree with the basic premise behind the calculations made for *Limits*. A time will come, they agree, when Earth's gold, copper, coal, and other resources will be depleted.

The case presented in *The Global 2000 Report* is typical. *Global 2000* was a report prepared for President Jimmy Carter in 1980.[28] It was described in *The Resourceful Earth* as an "official American perspective on the world economy in the 1980s."[29] The report was intended to be very influential. More than a million copies were printed and distributed and it was translated into five foreign languages. The report warned that "serious stresses involving population, resources, and environment are clearly visible ahead."

Most optimists, on the other hand, argue that a situation that seems perfectly clear in theory is not confirmed by what is happening in the real world. Simon bases his argument, for example, on what we mean by the term *scarcity*. In one sense, people talk about a resource as "scarce" if there isn't much of it. In those terms, pure gold is scarce in most of our lives.

But to an economist, however, scarcity is measured in dollars and cents. If an item is scarce, people are willing to pay a high price for it. If the item is not scarce, the item has a low monetary value. One can measure the scarcity of resources, then, by measuring their price.

On that basis, Optimists say that natural resources are not becoming scarcer. Indeed, some are becoming less scarce all the time! In a chapter for Simon and Kahn's book on *The Resourceful Earth*, Harold J. Barnett and his co-authors pointed out that the price of nine essential minerals showed a decline between 1950 and 1980, the price of one other mineral stayed the same, and the price of four showed increases. They concluded that "cost trend evidence for non-fuel minerals fails to support the increasing scarcity hypothesis."[30] In other words, if you measure scarcity by price, most minerals did not become scarcer between 1950 and 1980.

OPTIMIST VS. PESSIMIST

One of the most fascinating side stories of the ongoing overpopulation debate dates to 1980, when Paul Ehrlich (a Pessimist) and Julian Simon (an Optimist) agreed to a bet as to whether the world was, in fact, running out of natural resources or not. They chose five metals—chromium, copper, nickel, tin, and tungsten—as the basis for their bet. Ehrlich wagered that the price of these metals would increase over the next decade because they would become scarcer. Simon placed his money on the belief that, at the end of the bet period, the metals would cost less because people had found new supplies of them.

In fact, Simon won that bet, although the factors that produced his success were actually quite complicated, and most economists agree that Ehrlich could have won the wager if conditions were just a bit different than they actually were during the decade.[31]

ARE THERE ADEQUATE LAND RESOURCES?

As the 1980s drew to a close, Pessimists were especially concerned about the loss of land resources. According to one study, 77% of the world's arable land had already been at least moderately degraded. One third had lost at least a quarter of its productivity.[32]

The amount of available arable land is important, of course, since it at least partly determines the amount of food crops that can be grown. By one estimate, soil erosion was responsible for $1 billion in lost crops annually during the 1980s.[33]

The cause of land damage, Pessimists claim, is the world's ever-growing population. People are using agricultural methods that place too great a demand on the land. In some cases, farming is done on lands that cannot produce crops the way farmers want. Even arable land is endangered as farmers push harder to increase productivity from soil with limited capability.

As a result, increasing amounts of land are being converted to deserts. In the United Nations Population Fund report for 1988, Special Envoy to the United Nations Secretary General, Nafis Sadik, claimed that "The spread of the desert is one reason for Africa's failure to match overall population growth with food production."[34]

The desertification of land comes about primarily in one of four ways. First, overgrazing by domesticated animals removes plant cover. Soil is first exposed and then eroded by wind and water. Second, croplands are over-cultivated. Scientifically dependable techniques for letting land "rest" and regain its lost nutrients or supplying those nutrients through other means are either not known to or are ignored by farmers. Thus, after a few years, once productive farmland loses its ability to support plant growth. Again, bare soil is eroded.

Third, land is damaged by improper irrigation techniques. If land is not properly drained, the water table rises. Crop roots become anchored in saturated soil. Eventually the roots rot and the plants die. Also, as irrigation water evaporates, it leaves salts behind on the soil. Over time,

Brazil has seen massive deforestation in recent years. Loss of trees harms the soil and reduces the amount of natural resources available.

these salts accumulate and eventually the soil becomes too salty to support plant life. The land can no longer be used for farming. Finally, destruction of forests also leads to the loss of land. Tree roots hold huge volumes of water in the soil. When the trees are cut down, the soil in which they were growing dries out. Again, the soil is washed or blown away.

Optimists are generally less concerned about the loss of land resources. They agree that any nation, like any good farmer, has an obligation to take care of its resources. But, as Simon argued, there is no evidence that the world is likely to run out of farmland in the foreseeable future. All statistics suggest, he said, that the amount of arable land has actually increased over the past few decades and is likely to continue to do so in the future. He cites statistics from the United Nations Food and Agriculture Organization showing that, between 1961 and 1975, the amount of farmland increased worldwide from 1,403 to 1,507 million hectares.[35]

In Africa, for example, the fraction of the continent's land in productive use increased from 32.88% in 1966 to 33.29% in 1975. Similar increases were observed in the Far East, Middle East, and Latin America. Only in the MDCs did the fraction of land devoted to farming decrease, from 25.85% to 25.50% in North America, and from 44.83% to 43.72% in Western Europe.[36]

The downward trend, Simon argued, illustrates the efficiency of modem agriculture. Farmers have learned how to increase crop yield with fertilizers, machinery, and other modern techniques. Thus, they can grow more food on the same or even less land. This fact is a good sign for the LDCs, the Optimists say. Even if the amount of farmland should decrease, agriculture will not necessarily suffer. By using the best technology available, LDCs can also produce more food on the same or smaller plots of land.

POLLUTION ISSUES

Most people today would probably be willing to admit that pollution is an important social problem. But who or what causes the problem of pollution? How can it be reduced? And is it getting worse or less severe? It is on those questions that people are likely to disagree.

During the 1970s, many Pessimists argued that population growth was a major cause of increasing pollution. If ten people cause a certain level of pollution, the argument went, then one hundred people would cause at least ten times as much pollution. In MDCs, the effect was thought to be even more serious. With their high standard of living, ten Americans or ten Canadians probably caused much more pollution than did ten Zambians or ten Nigerians. The population-pollution connection, then, was one of special concern to MDCs.

In 1971, for example, the Campaign to Check the Population Explosion published a full-page advertisement in many US newspapers. The ad claimed that "people pollute!" After describing the scope and cost of the nation's pollution problems, the ad pointed out: "Even this vast expenditure [i.e., the projected cost of cleaning up pollution in the United States] will not stop pollution unless we check the rapid growth of our population."[37]

Many observers have argued that this view is too simplistic. They say that pollution results from a combination of population and technology factors. Humans pollute not only because there are so many of them, but also because of the many new inventions they have produced. Moreover, population contributes to pollution problems primarily when people are crowded together in urban areas. Thus, the combination of population and pollution are likely to be most serious in the world's large urban areas such as Mexico City, Sao Paulo, New York, and London.

Optimists view the issue of pollution differently. In the first place, pollution trends, they say, are neither clear nor consistent. In some ways, our environment is cleaner than it was fifty years ago, although in other ways, it is dirtier. And pollution problems differ dramatically from one nation to another, from one state to another, from one city to another. Even though population has continued to grow throughout the world over the last century, levels of pollution simply do not correspond to rates of population growth.[38]

Julian Simon presented a familiar argument on this issue. For one thing, he said, a larger population means a greater number of intelligent people in a society. Thus, the chances are better that someone will know how to solve pollution problems than in a smaller population.

Of greater importance, however, is the fact that solving pollution problems is more a political, social, and economic issue than a population issue. When people have the will to clean up the environment, they act to do that. In the United States, for example, the government passed the Clean Air Act and Water Pollution Control Act. These acts forced polluters to "clean up their act." Environmental quality improves not because there are fewer people, but because of social pressures.[39]

In its 1986 report on population growth and economic development, the National Research Council supported that view. It suggested that countries act against pollution when resources such as air, water, and land are seriously threatened. Although slower population growth may allow countries more time to act on pollution, population growth itself may be of limited significance in controlling pollution.[40]

In the early 1990s, experts began to express greater concern about one specific form of environmental damage: changes in the atmosphere.

Evidence began to accumulate that human activities were starting to deplete the ozone layer in Earth's stratosphere and to increase the atmosphere's annual average temperatures (the greenhouse effect). Data on these two effects were both questionable and incomplete. But more and more authorities thought that population growth might be a critical factor in producing potentially dangerous changes in the atmosphere. (See the section on climate change, p. 122)

For some authorities, concern about atmospheric changes produced a decisive tilt in their attitudes about population growth. They feared that more people living in more technological societies could only contribute to damaging Earth's atmosphere.

As usual, Julian Simon and other Optimists have not been very worried about atmospheric changes. The technology for solving these problems already exists, they point out. The only question, suggested, for example, by *New York Times* columnist Peter Passell is: When will Earth's peoples be willing to pay the price for dealing with these problems?[41]

QUALITY OF LIFE

At least since the time of Thomas Malthus, one of the most fundamental arguments of population Pessimists has been that human misery is an "absolutely necessary consequence" of population growth.[42] That conclusion was an essential feature of Malthus's argument in his "Essay," and many people are likely to agree with the statement today. We think of nations with rapidly growing populations, and we imagine people living in poverty, hunger, and disease. We picture rapidly growing urban areas, and we expect to see slums that offer the lowest possible standard of living.

Malthus's statement makes some sense logically. As population grows, the amount of food, coal, iron, and other resources for each person decreases. A larger population means a reduced standard of living for each individual person. Kingsley Davis, father of the ZPG movement, has warned that current population growth will lead to the "global standard of living we now have in Bangladesh or the poorest places in Africa."[43] Even without thinking about it, we may be inclined to agree with the Worldwatch Institute's conclusion that "rapid population growth and social progress are not compatible in the long term," and that nations with growing populations "may now face a choice: Adopt a one-child family goal or accept a decline in living standards."[44]

The second of these statements shows the practical significance of this idea. If slower population growth leads to a higher standard of living, then birth control measures (the one-child family, for example) may be a valid national goal. Is the connection between population growth and quality of life this simple, though? Is it a fact that rapid population growth leads to a decline in standard of living? The answers that seem so obvious, however, may or may not be true, and experts are likely to disagree about the actual state of affairs. Our thinking may be influenced as much by slogans as by facts. In 1986, for example, popular science writer John Tierney expressed the belief that "population growth is merely the most convenient excuse for failure—one that doesn't put the blame on socialists, capitalists, African politicians, or foreign aid donors."[45]

What, indeed, are the facts about population growth and quality of life? In fact, the connection between these two situations is not at all clear in the real world. Certainly, the experience of many LDCs today seems to confirm that growing populations lead to a reduced standard

Until recently, China enforced a one-child policy for many of its citizens in an effort to curb population growth. The policy has since been relaxed, but that country still faces major population challenges.

of living. Reports from Asia, Latin America. and Africa, all countries with high population growth, suggest a connection with widespread poverty, hunger, and overall misery.[46]

Robert McNamara, former president of the World Bank, has coined the term *absolute poverty* for the most destitute of the world's poor. By "absolute poverty" he means "a condition of life so characterized by malnutrition, illiteracy and disease as to be beneath any reasonable definition of human decency."[47] By one 1990 estimate, more than one billion people live in absolute poverty.[48]

Optimists, of course, have a very different take on the question of population growth and quality of life. In his book *Theory of Population and Economic Growth*, Julian Simon made a case for why population growth may lead to an improved standard of living. He stated that nations with fast-growing populations may have short-term problems. Famine and misery may occur during the early stages of population growth. But eventually, he argued, new technology, a greater number of creative people, and increased demand will lead to a better life for the average person.[49]

The 1986 National Research Council (NRC) report tends to support this view. That report emphasized how different situations are from country to country. Conditions in Kenya are very different from those in Nigeria, its neighbor. Any statements about population growth and standard of living in Kenya probably have little to do with the situation in Nigeria.

Overall, the NRC believes that "slower population growth would be beneficial to economic development for most developing countries." The effect, however, is likely to be modest. Reducing population growth is certainly not likely to "vault a typical developing country into the ranks of the developed."[50]

The chairman of the NRC study has written that "the process of economic growth can be mildly accelerated through family planning programs [that is, through reduced population growth]." But, he warned, we should understand that "there is little evidence to support the extreme claims that population growth is either an 'unmitigated disaster' or a 'boon to human well-being.'"[51]

OVERPOPULATION VERSUS OVERCONSUMPTION

The debate in this chapter thus far has focused almost entirely on one key question: To what extent are the world's problems of hunger, natural resources, climate change, quality of life, and the like a result of there being too many people on Earth? The basic argument by

In 2012 the Philippines passed a Reproductive Health Bill aimed at reducing population through birth control and increased education. Many developing countries (LDCs) have been called upon to reduce fertility and birth rates.

population Pessimists is that most or all of these problems are a result of unacceptably large increases in population. They have argued that as more and more children are born, as the human population continues to increase unabated, problems such as hunger, disease, shortages of fresh water, loss of natural habitat and extinction of species, and global climate change will continue to become more serious. The only long-term solution for dealing with such problems, they often say, is to reduce population growth.

That philosophy places the responsibility of solving the world's environmental, social, health, and other problems squarely in the hands of the less developed nations. They are the places, after all, where population numbers continue to grow out of control. Compare the total fertility rate in 2014 in Chad (6.3 children per woman) or Mali (6.8 children per woman) to the same rate in Austria or Germany or Japan (all 1.4 children per woman), and it's obvious whose "fault" it is that the earth is overpopulated: those countries with high fertility and birth rates.[52]

So it's hardly surprising that much of the talk about controlling population and reducing the problems caused by overpopulation has long focused on ways of getting LDCs to cut back on their total fertility rates and birth rates. Nearly every conference ever held on population control seems to start or end with calls by the world's rich and well-developed nations calling on the world's poorest and least-developed nations to find ways of cutting back on their population control.

But experts have long recognized that overpopulation is only part of the reason that the world is now suffering from a host of problems like those described in the previous chapter. Another important issue is overconsumption. The term *overconsumption* has been defined in a variety

TAKE ACTION!

What is your community doing to reduce overconsumption of essential resources? Speak with your local city or county commissioner or other administrative officer to find out the answer to that question. Prepare a visual display that will summarize what you have learned about the specific resource (food, water, trees, land, energy, etc.) for which your community has sustainability plans. Make your display available in print or electronically for the community as a whole with a mechanism by which they can respond to the information that you collected.

As a second part of your project, think of a second resource available to your community for which there is as yet no sustainability plan. Prepare a plan for submission to local officials that outline an approach that your community can take to reduce unnecessary consumption of that resource.

of ways, but it usually refers to the situation in which humans use up resources faster than they can be produced or at a rate that is not sustainable. There are a plethora of examples today of the ways that humans are overconsuming our natural resources. One such example involves the overfishing of the world's oceans. For centuries, humans have taken many varieties of fish from the ocean, acting under the assumption that there would always be enough fish to feed everyone who wanted fish. Very few people, until recent decades, have ever imagined that humans would "run out of fish."

Yet, just that result has begun to occur for many food species of fish. For example, the peak recorded catch of Atlantic cod was recorded in

1968, when 3.9 million tons of the fish were taken by anglers. By 1992 that number had fallen to 1.2 million tons, a decline of 69 percent. Similar stories can be told for other food fish, such as South African pilchard (a decrease of 94 percent during the period from 1968 to 1992), Polar cod (a decrease of 94 percent from 1972 to 1992), and silver hake (a decrease of 88 percent from 1973 to 1992).[53]

These numbers cast a somewhat different light on the discussion of overpopulation. After all, it is usually not the poorest communities that send out massive fishing fleets to denude the oceans of food fish; it is

TAKE ACTION!

One of the most troubling consequences of overconsumption by humans may be global climate change. Make a list of the specific actions that you and your family take every day on a regular basis that might contribute to global climate change in one way or another. Prepare an Action Plan that outlines the specific steps you and your family can take to reduce your contribution to global climate change. Follow your plan for a week to see how it affects the way you live your life on a day-to-day basis. Write a brief statement that summarizes your views on "How One Person Can Have an Effect on Global Climate Change."

Repeat this exercise for some group of individuals with whom you are involved, such as your class at school, the team you work with outside of school, a church group, or any club or student organization to which you may belong. What specific actions can the members of this group take to have an effect on global climate change? Talk with other members of your group to think of a way in which to convey the findings of this study to other members of the community.

Many people are aware of the role MDCs play in depleting the oceans of fish. Protesters against overfishing demonstrate in Brussels, Belgium, on May 13, 2013 during a meeting of the EU Agriculture and Fisheries Council.

usually large commercial fishing fleets owned and/or operated by companies in the United States, United Kingdom, China, Japan, Australia, or some other developed nation. That point is that the people who live in MDCs and their governments have at least as much responsibility for dealing with Earth's many environmental, social, economic, and political problems as do LDCs with high birth and total fertility rates.

OVERPOPULATION AND CLIMATE CHANGE

At the middle of the second decade of the twenty first century, two major problems are meeting head-on across the globe: overpopulation and climate change. Yet, relatively little discussion has been occurring about this clash of issues. Why is the threat of a growing world population to

TAKE ACTION!

Imagine that you have been asked to teach a lesson to a ninth-grade biology class about the connection between population growth and climate change. Collect as much information as you can about this topic and prepare a thirty-minute lesson that shows why increasing numbers of humans on the planet can affect climate patterns. Remember that your class may know very little about population growth or about climate change, so keep your presentation simple. Use graphs, pictures, videos, or any other visual tools that will make your presentation easier to understand. At the end of your presentation, ask your listeners to suggest actions that they themselves, their families, and friends can take to deal with the threat posed by overpopulation to Earth's climate. (Be prepared with your own list of suggestions in case class members need some prompting to get started on this part of the lesson.)

the planet's survival escaping the notice of experts in the area, as well as that of everyday citizens?

To begin with, what is the connection between overpopulation and climate change? Many experts today now acknowledge the fact that growing numbers of humans will inevitably lead to an increase in the amount of greenhouse gases released to Earth's atmosphere and, hence, an increase in the planet's average annual temperature: global warming. A 2008 study conducted by researchers at Oregon State University, for example, found that the amount of carbon dioxide produced by each new child born in the United States was about twenty times as much as could be saved by an individual's adopting a host of carbon-saving activities, such as recycling and driving a high-mileage car. The researchers concluded that "the potential savings from reduced reproduction are huge compared to the savings that can be achieved by changes in lifestyle."[54]

Once more, the solution to this problem might be to have LDCs reduce their birth rates, thus reducing the number of children who will contribute to global climate change. But that argument holds no water for the simple reason that children born in affluent MDCs use far more natural resources per person than do those born in LDCs. So combating global warming means reducing birth rates both in LDCs and in MDCs with high birth rates, most notably, the United States.

With this type of future a possibility, why are politicians and many experts in the field so reluctant to talk about the connection between overpopulation and climate change? The answer is an old one: No country likes to be told that it has to adopt policies forcing families to have fewer children than they want to have. That challenge is especially difficult when

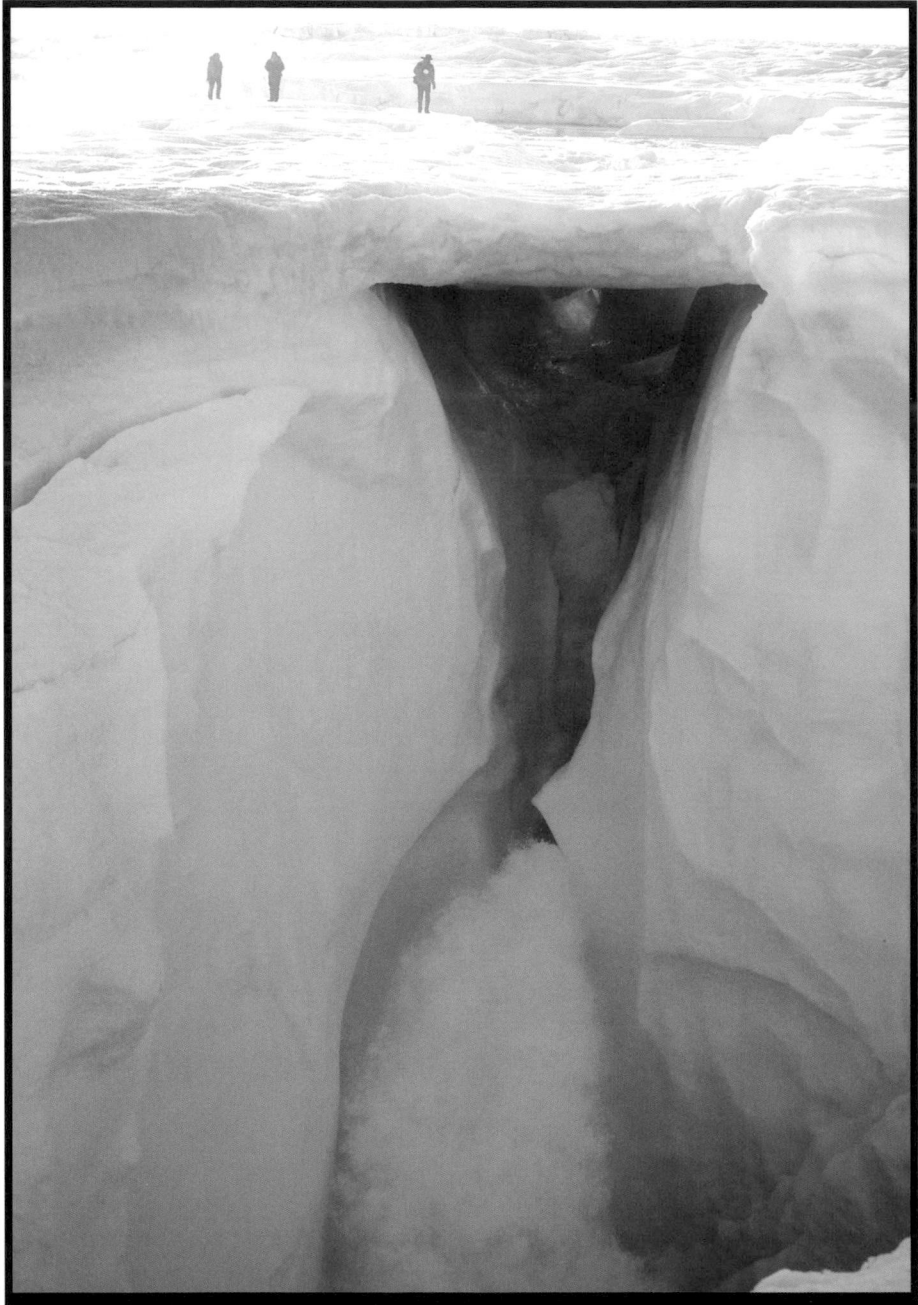

The melting ice sheet in Greenland is one sign of global warming.
Some experts maintain that overpopulation has led to increased levels
of greenhouse gases, which in turn has led to climate change.

it comes to having rich MDCs telling poor LDCs that they need to cut back on population growth that those countries may see as essential to their own development.[55] The solution, some observers suggest, lies in better education for citizens of all nations about the environmental benefits of voluntary birth control programs that not only help to bring population growth under control, but also hold promise for dealing with some of the world's most serious environmental problems, such as climate change.

CHAPTER 8

ONE SOLUTION: POPULATION CONTROL?

THE LAST THREE CHAPTERS HAVE PRESENTED MANY different views on the question of overpopulation. Some people feel that rapid population growth is cause for celebration. Others think it is a disaster.

Consider the situation in Kenya. Its total fertility rate (TFR) in 1988 was 4.1%, the highest in the world and one of the highest ever recorded for a single nation. (Remember that total fertility rate is the average number of children born to a woman during her lifetime.) Julian Simon's response to that fact was: "Isn't it wonderful that so many people can be alive in that country today?"[1] On the other side, journalist Pranay Gupte claimed that "rampant population growth" in Kenya was "holding back the country's social and economic progress." The nation lacked the leaders it needed, he said, "to save itself" from its population problems.[2]

Much of what you have read so far involves unknown and uncertain factors. The United Nations can report the amount of wheat grown in

The growing number of people in the world is seen as favorable by some, and a problematic by others. Here a mother holds her child in Kenya, a country whose population continues to grow thanks to decreased infant mortality and increased life expectancy.

Zambia last year, for example. But people can then disagree as to what these numbers mean. As you have seen, Optimists and Pessimists argue back and forth as to what we should do—if anything—about rapid population growth.

This chapter has less to do with what people have to say about population growth and more with what they do about it. The contrast is quite striking. In the early 1980s, most nations had lined up on the side of the Pessimists. In 1982, by one estimate, seventy-two of the world's LDCs, representing 94% of the people living in LDCs, supported some form of population control.[3]

The term *population control* refers to any effort by a government to control the size of its population. Sometimes a nation tries to *increase* its population. For example, a small country may feel that it can be more powerful if it has more people, so it may try to encourage population growth. More commonly, though, a nation worries that its population is too large or that it is growing too fast. In that case, it may act to reduce population growth.

How does a nation control the size of its population? In theory, it could try to alter its birth rate, death rate, rate of immigration, or rate of emigration. In fact, however, population control nearly always involves only the first of these, the birth rate.

People often think of birth control as limiting the number of births, but *control* does not have to mean "limit" or "slow." It can also mean "decide." For example, a couple may decide that they want to have three children. At first, they might have to find ways to increase the chance of having a child. Or they may reach a point where they want to avoid having more children.

Some population experts prefer the term *family planning* to *birth control*. *Family planning* is used to describe any program that allows parents to have the number of children they want.

A STORY WITH TWO SIDES

Suppose a nation wants to increase its population. In practice, that means the government will look for ways to encourage more births. This kind of policy is called *pronatalist* (*pro*: "in favor of"; *natalist*, "birth").

Pronatalist governments can be found throughout history. For example, the first Christian emperor of Rome, Constantine, tried to encourage marriage and child-bearing by giving special preferences in government jobs to married men and fathers. Mothers of three or more children wore special clothing, which allowed the general public to recognize and honor them. In contrast, unmarried and childless men faced various penalties, including having to pay special taxes that married men and fathers did not.[4]

Germany also had a pronatalist policy during the period of National Socialism (Nazism). Martin Bormann, Adolf Hitler's third deputy, encouraged German men to help the nation recover from wartime losses by "having as many children as possible." The Nazi plan was not only to encourage population growth, but also to "purify" the nation. Members of the Schutzstaffel (SS) were given leave to have intercourse with women who had been selected for their "correct" Aryan characteristics.[5]

Few nations in the world today have pronatalist policies, with Ireland being one exception. The Irish see people as a valuable national resource. An ad produced by the Industrial Development Authority proclaimed, in fact, that "People are to Ireland as champagne is to France." The ad

One of Hitler's closest advisors, Martin Bormann advocated procreation as a way to ensure that the Aryan race remain dominant in Germany.

boasts about the benefits Ireland has of having "Europe's youngest and fastest growing population."[6]

The United States has never developed a national policy for increasing, decreasing, or maintaining population size. Still, both presidential and legislative actions suggest that the US government tends to favor a pronatalist stand.

Married people, for example, receive an income tax deduction for children, one way of rewarding people for having children. Also, the presidential administrations of Ronald Reagan and George Bush opposed legalized abortion. Although they almost certainly did not take this position for population reasons, since abortion is a major method of reducing births, the presidents' position was a pronatalist stance.

Both the Reagan and Bush administrations took a pronatalist position in their international policies as well. From 1984, they prohibited the use of US tax dollars for birth control programs administered by the United Nations. In contrast to Ireland and the United States, most nations today favor some form of antinatalism, which refers to any effort by a nation to slow population growth by limiting the number of births.

One of the world's best-known antinatalist policy is that of China. In the 1960s, Chinese officials began to worry about the nation's population growth. Experts predicted that the then-current birth rates would cause a growth in population from 400 million in 1962 to at least 1.2 billion by the year 2000. The government regarded this growth rate as unacceptable. It would slow economic growth, produce widespread hunger and misery, and cause terrible environmental damage, officials believed.

Reflecting this concern, the Chinese government implemented what has become known as its "one-child policy," limiting families to having no

China's strict one-child policy was recently amended to allow families to have a second child if one spouse is an only child.

more than one child per family. That restriction had a number of exceptions, and as recently as 2007, only about a third of the nation's married couples were subject to the policy. By 2014 the Chinese government had finally changed its mind, and announced a much less restrictive policy, with many couples being allowed a second child, provided they made application to do so. Interestingly, many fewer couples actually did apply to have a second child than the government had anticipated.

The Chinese program is only one kind of antinatalism. Other nations have developed other kinds of antinatalist programs. In the 1950s, India attempted to stem the population growth through sterilization. Today, a more moderate program has been put in place that aims to educate women in particular about health and contraception. In Iran, couples are encouraged to have fewer children, with the government covering most family planning costs.

Given the vastly different circumstances among the countries of the world, it is safe to assume that we will continue to see a wide array of approaches to population growth. Ultimately, each nation assesses the state of its people, its economy, its environment, and decides on the course of action it believes will ensure future prosperity.

EPILOGUE

THE ISSUE OF POPULATION GROWTH INVOLVES SOME of the most difficult and controversial questions facing the world today, many of which have arisen because of progress in medical science. Untold millions of people are alive today who would have died of disease only a hundred years ago. While no one questions the benefits of medical progress, lower death rates create new population issues for nations around the world.

The immediate consequence of lower death rates is a growing population, since women continue to have children at relatively high rates. But instead of dying at an early age, those children survive and add to a country's population. As living standards in a society improve, the birth rate then usually begins to turn downward. Any concerns about excess population seem to disappear in the natural course of events. Today, in many developed countries of the world, governments are more concerned about having too few people than too many.

Less developed countries, on the other hand, often face a quite different issue. They have to find ways to feed, house, educate, and care for a population whose growth still seems out of control. How can they survive, some ask, until improved living conditions bring about that "natural" decrease in birth rates and, ultimately, population stabilization?

Perhaps the most difficult issue of all involves the effects of population growth. Are growing populations a desirable trend, as many economists suggest? Or do they lead to depletion of natural resources, increasing levels of pollution and the general misery of the "overpopulated" nations, as biologists and other observers think?

The complexity of the issues involved stems from the fact that dealing with them requires government intervention into the most personal aspects of human life: sexual reproduction. Does a government have the right to tell a man and woman how many children they should have? When do the needs of society become more important than the rights of individuals? How far can a nation go to impose its ideas about population growth on its citizens?

Some people argue that the very survival of the world—or, at least, of some nations in it—is at stake. They believe that population problems must be solved before we can work on the world's many other problems. Others say that the role of population growth—up or down—in such problems is unproved, and probably irrelevant. They believe that the world would be no better off—even probably worse off—if humans tried to tinker with the process of family planning.

Population issues address, therefore, the most fundamental ways in which humans relate to their governments. It is hardly surprising that debates over population growth are often highly emotional. This can make it difficult to find the facts about population growth one must have to make informed decisions about the best actions to take. But the only way to finally make sense out of the world's population situation is to persevere in that search for truth. Even as we read vivid stories of the world's end—in a blaze of glory or a blaze of disaster—we must always look for the facts. Only in that way can we ever hope to find the best way or ways to deal with population issues.

APPENDIX

EXCERPT FROM "WORLD URBANIZATION PROSPECT,"

United Nations, Department of Economic and Social Affairs, 2014:

WORLD URBANIZATION TRENDS 2014: KEY FACTS

Globally, more people live in urban areas than in rural areas, with 54 per cent of the world's population residing in urban areas in 2014. In 1950, 30 per cent of the world's population was urban, and by 2050, 66 per cent of the world's population is projected to be urban.

Today, the most urbanized regions include Northern America (82 per cent living in urban areas in 2014), Latin America and the Caribbean (80 per cent), and Europe (73 per cent). In contrast, Africa and Asia remain mostly rural, with 40 and 48 per cent of their respective populations living in urban areas. All regions are expected to urbanize further over the coming decades. Africa and Asia are urbanizing faster than the other regions and are projected to become 56 and 64 per cent urban, respectively, by 2050.

The rural population of the world has grown slowly since 1950 and is expected to reach its peak in a few years. The global rural population is now close to 3.4 billion and is expected to decline to 3.2 billion by 2050. Africa and Asia are home to nearly 90 per cent of the world's rural population. India has the largest rural population (857 million), followed by China (635 million).

The urban population of the world has grown rapidly since 1950, from 746 million to 3.9 billion in 2014. Asia, despite its lower level of urbanization, is home to 53 per cent of the world's urban population, followed by Europe (14 per cent) and Latin America and the Caribbean (13 per cent).

Continuing population growth and urbanization are projected to add 2.5 billion people to the world's urban population by 2050, with nearly 90 per cent of the increase concentrated in Asia and Africa.

Just three countries—India, China and Nigeria—together are expected to account for 37 per cent of the projected growth of the world's urban population between 2014 and 2050. India is projected to add 404 million urban dwellers, China 292 million and Nigeria 212 million.

Close to half of the world's urban dwellers reside in relatively small settlements of less than 500,000 inhabitants, while only around one in eight live in the 28 mega-cities with more than 10 million inhabitants.

Tokyo is the world's largest city with an agglomeration of 38 million inhabitants, followed by Delhi with 25 million, Shanghai with 23 million, and Mexico City, Mumbai and São Paulo, each with around 21 million inhabitants. By 2030, the world is projected to have 41 mega-cities with more than 10 million inhabitants. Tokyo is projected to remain the world's largest city in 2030 with 37 million inhabitants, followed closely by Delhi where the population is projected to rise swiftly to 36 million. Several decades ago most of the world's largest urban agglomerations were found in the more developed regions, but today's large cities are concentrated in the global South. The fastest growing urban agglomerations are medium-sized cities and cities with less than 1 million inhabitants located in Asia and Africa.

Some cities have experienced population decline in recent years. Most of these are located in the low-fertility countries of Asia and Europe where the overall population is stagnant or declining. Economic contraction and natural disasters have contributed to population losses in some cities as well.

As the world continues to urbanize, sustainable development challenges will be increasingly concentrated in cities, particularly in the lower-middle-income countries where the pace of urbanization is fastest. Integrated policies to improve the lives of both urban and rural dwellers are needed.

To view the report in its entirety, go to:

http://esa.un.org/unpd/wup/Highlights/WUP2014-Highlights.pdf

Excerpts from "World at War," United Nations High Commissioner for Refugees (UNHCR), 2014:

INTRODUCTION

Global forced displacement has seen accelerated growth in 2014, once again reaching unprecedented levels. The year saw the highest displacement on record. By end-2014, 59.5 million individuals were forcibly displaced worldwide as a result of persecution, conflict, generalized violence, or human rights violations. This is 8.3 million persons more than the year before (51.2 million) and the highest annual increase in a single year.

The year 2014 has seen continuing dramatic growth in mass displacement from wars and conflict, once again reaching levels unprecedented in recent history. One year ago, UNHCR announced that worldwide forced displacement numbers had reached 51.2 million, a level not previously seen in the post-World War II era. Twelve months later, this figure has grown to a staggering 59.5 million, roughly equaling the population of Italy or the United Kingdom. Persecution, conflict, generalized violence, and human rights violations have formed a 'nation of the displaced' that, if they were a country, would make up the 24th largest in the world.

During this year of spiralling crises, with millions of people already forced to flee from their homes and many thousands dying while trying to get to safety, the global humanitarian system has been severely stretched. New crises have broken out in the Middle East and Africa, compounded by continuing unresolved conflicts in Afghanistan, the Democratic Republic of the Congo, Somalia, and elsewhere. In addition to the ongoing crisis in the Syrian Arab Republic, new conflicts in the Central African Republic, South Sudan, Ukraine, and Iraq, among others, have caused suffering and massive displacement. As a consequence, the combined number of refugees and internally displaced persons protected/assisted by UNHCR in 2014 increased by 11.0 million persons, reaching a record high of 46.7 million persons by year end.

It is not just the scale of global forced displacement that is disconcerting but also its rapid acceleration in recent years. For most of the past decade, displacement figures ranged between 38 million and 43 million persons annually. Since 2011, however, when levels stood at 42.5 million, these numbers have grown to the current 59.5 million—a 40 per cent increase within a span of just three years.

Such growth poses challenges to finding adequate responses to these crises, increasingly leading to the multiple displacement of individuals or secondary movements in search of safety.

In Europe, more than 219,000 refugees and migrants crossed the Mediterranean Sea during 2014.

That's almost three times the previously known high of about 70,000, which took place in 2011 during the 'Arab Spring'. Nearly half of these arrivals were coming from the Syrian Arab Republic and Eritrea. UNHCR has received information of over 3,500 women, men, and children reported dead or missing in the Mediterranean Sea during the year, clearly demonstrating how dangerous and unpredictable this situation has become.

While 2.9 million persons sought refuge abroad, mostly in neighbouring countries, 11.0 million were displaced within the borders of their countries. In addition, a record high of nearly 1.7 million persons lodged asylum claims on an individual basis during 2014. Conflict and persecution thus forced an average of 42,500 persons per day to leave their homes in 2014. This compares to 32,200 one year ago and constitutes a four-fold increase since 2010 (10,900).

To read the full report, go to:

http://unhcr.org/556725e69.html#_ga=1.225701913.2095888809.1417795315

CHAPTER NOTES

Chapter 1. The Population Explosion

1. "Indian Baby Picked as World's 'Seven Billionth' Person," *The Hindu*, accessed June 18, 2015, http://www.thehindu.com/news/national/birth-of-nargis-raises-hopes-fears-for-nations-future/article2586156.ece.

2. Central Intelligence Agency, "Somalia," *The World Factbook*, accessed June 18, 2015, https://www.cia.gov/library/publications/the-world-factbook/geos/so.html.

3. Maja Pearce, Adewale, and Eleanor Whitehead, "Factsheet: Nigeria's Population Figures," *Africa Check*, accessed June 18, 2015, http://africacheck.org/factsheets/factsheet-nigerias-population-figures/.

4. Schlesinger, Robert, "The 2015 U.S. and World Populations," *U.S. News and World Report*, accessed June 18, 2015, http://www.usnews.com/opinion/blogs/robert-schlesinger/2014/12/31/us-population-2015-320-million-and-world-population-72-billion.

Chapter 2. Measuring Population Trends

1. Mona Chalabi, "How Many Times Does the Average Person Move?" *Five Thirty Eight*, accessed June 19, 2015, http://fivethirtyeight.com/datalab/how-many-times-the-average-person-moves/.

2. William Petersen, *Population*, 3rd ed. (New York: Macmillan Publishing Company, 1975), 494.

3. United Nations, Department of Economic and Social Affairs, Population Division, *World Urbanization Prospects: The 2014 Revision, Highlights* (New York: The United Nations, 2014).

4. "World at War. UNHCR Global Trends. Forced Displacement in 2014," accessed June 19, 2015, http://unhcr.org/556725e69.html#_ga=1.225701913.2095888809.1417795315.

5. "As Thousands Continue to Flee Myanmar, UNHCR Concerned about Growing Reports of Abuse," *UNHCR*, accessed June 19, 2015, http://www.unhcr.org/5396ee3b9.html.

6. "5 Facts about Illegal Immigration in the U.S.," Pew Research Center, accessed June 23, 2015, http://www.pewresearch.org/fact-tank/2014/11/18/5-facts-about-illegal-immigration-in-the-u-s/.

7. "Chapter 2: Birthplaces of U.S. Unauthorized Immigrants," Pew Research Center, accessed June 23, 2015, http://www.pewhispanic.org/2014/11/18/chapter-2-birthplaces-of-u-s-unauthorized-immigrants/.

Chapter 3. The Demographic Transition

1. "The 20 Countries with the Highest Population Growth Rate in 2014," *Statista*, accessed June 20, 2015, http://www.statista.com/statistics/264687/countries-with-the-highest-population-growth-rate/.

2. Colin McEvedy and Richard Jones, *Atlas of World Population History* (Harmondsworth, Middlesex, England: Penguin Books, 1985), 34.

3. Ibid., 172.

4. William Petersen, *Population*, 3rd ed. (New York: Macmillan Publishing Company, 1975), 269.

5. John Keegan, "Lessons of History's Bloodiest Battle." *U.S. News & World Report*, August 1, 1988, 31.

6. Petersen, 420.

7. Kingsley Davis, *The Population of India and Pakistan* (Princeton, NJ: Princeton University Press, 1951), 39.

8. "Starvation as a Political Weapon." *U.S. News & World Report*, February 6, 1989, 34–35.

9. Mary Battiata, "Plenty of Food-Sudanese Still Starving," *San Francisco Chronicle*, October 17, 1988, A l7.

10. For further information on the Black Death, see Petersen, 422; McEvedy and Jones, 25; and William L. Langer, "The Black Death," *Scientific American*, February 1964, 114–121.

11. "Mortality Slide Series," National Center for HIV/AIDS, Slide 4, accessed June 20, 2015, http://www.cdc.gov/hiv/pdf/statistics_surveillance_hiv_mortality.pdf.

12. "HIV/AIDS," Global Health Observatory (GBO) Data, World Health Organization, accessed June 20, 2015, http://www.who.int/gho/hiv/en/.

13. "Mortality Rate, Infant (per 1,000 Live Births)," The World Bank, accessed June 22, 2015, http://data.worldbank.org/indicator/SP.DYN.IMRT.IN.

Chapter 4. Population Issues in North America

1. *Encyclopedia Americana* (Danbury, CT: Grolier, 1989), vol. 15, 1.

2. Ibid., 318.

3. *Encyclopedia Americana* (Danbury, CT: Grolier, 1989), vol. 27, 523.

4. Ibid.

5. *Statistical Abstract of the United States-1990* (Washington, DC: Bureau of the Census, 1990), Table 7.

6. *Encyclopedia Americana* (Danbury, CT: Grolier, 1989), vol. 5, 316.

7. Gibson, Campbell, and Kay Jung. "Historical Census Statistics on Population Totals by Race, 1790 to 1990, and by Hispanic Origin, 1970 to 1990, For Large Cities and Other Urban Places in the United States," http://www.census.gov/population/www/documentation/twps0076/twps0076.pdf.

"Overview of Race and Hispanic Origin 2000." http://www.census.gov/prod/2001pubs/c2kbr01-1.pdf.

"Overview of Race and Hispanic Origin 2010." http://www.census.gov/prod/cen2010/briefs/c2010br-02.pdf.

https://en.wikipedia.org/wiki/Historical_racial_and_ethnic_demographics_of_the_United_States#Historical_data_for_all_races_and_for_Hispanic_origin_.281610.E2.80.932010

8. Gordon Sova, ed., *1991 Corpus Almanac & Canadian Sourcebook* (Don Mills, ON: Southam Business Information and Communications Group, 1991), 5-5.

9. "National Vital Statistics Report," Centers for Disease Control and Prevention, vol. 61, no 1, August 28, 2012, http://www.cdc.gov/nchs/data/nvsr/nvsr61/nvsr61_01.pdf.

10. "Overview of Race and Hispanic Origin: 2010," 2010 Census Briefs, accessed June 23, 2015, http://www.census.gov/prod/cen2010/briefs/c2010br-02.pdf.

11. "The Asian Population: 2010," 2010 Census Briefs, accessed June 23, 2015, https://www.census.gov/prod/cen2010/briefs/c2010br-11.pdf.

12. "Growth in Urban Population Outpaces Rest of Nation, Census Bureau Reports," United States Census Bureau, accessed June 23, 2015, https://www.census.gov/newsroom/releases/archives/2010_census/cb12-50.html.

Chapter 5. The Limits to Growth

1. Pentti Linkola, *Can Life Prevail? A Revolutionary Approach to the Environmental Crisis* (London: Arktos, 2011) 122.

2. David Osterfeld, "Overpopulation: The Perennial Myth," *The Freeman*, Foundation for Economic Education, September 1, 1993, http://fee.org/freeman/detail/overpopulation-the-perennial-myth.

3. "One Planet, How Many People? A Review of Earth's Carrying Capacity," *UNEP Global Environmental Alert Service*, June 2012, https://na.unep.net/geas/archive/pdfs/GEAS_Jun_12_Carrying_Capacity.pdf.

4. Garrett Hardin, "Cultural Carrying Capacity: A Biological Approach to Human Problems," *BioScience* 36 no. 9 (October 1986): 599–606.

5. Ibid., 603.

6. W. Jackson Davis, *The Seventh Year: Industrial Civilization in Transition* (New York: W. W. Norton, 1979), 228.

7. William Petersen, *Malthus: Founder of Modern Demography* (New Brunswick, NJ: Transaction Publishers, 1999), ch. 1.

8. T. R. Malthus and Geoffrey Gilbert, *An Essay on the Principle of Population* (Oxford; New York: Oxford University Press, 1999), 16.

9. Jeffrey Folks, "The Welfare State of the Union," *American Thinker*, February 10, 2011, http://www.americanthinker.com/articles/2011/02/the_welfare_state_of_the_union.html.

10. Sir John Boyd Orr, "Nothing to Worry About," in Hardin Garrett James, ed., *Population, Evolution, & Birth Control: A Collage of Controversial Readings* (San Francisco: W. H. Freeman, 1969), 56.

11. Dwight D. Eisenhower, "288—The President's News Conference, December 2, 1959," *The American Presidency Project*, accessed June 25, 2015, http://www.presidency.ucsb.edu/ws/?pid=11587.

12. Richard M. Nixon, "271—Special Message to the Congress on Problems of Population Growth, July 18, 1969," accessed June 25, 2015, http://www.presidency.ucsb.edu/ws/?pid=2132.

13. William Paddock and Paul Paddock, *Famine 1975! Who Will Survive?* (Boston: Little, Brown, 1967).

14. Paul Ehrlich, *The Population Bomb* (New York: Ballantine Books, 1968), xi.

15. Hardin, 1247.

16. "How Much Water Is on Earth?" The USGS Water Science School, last revised July 24, 2015, http://water.usgs.gov/edu/gallery/global-water-volume.html.

17. Richard C. Dorf, *The Energy Factbook* (New York: McGraw-Hill, 1981), 11, 53.

18. Donella H. Meadows et al., *The Limits to Growth* (New York: Universe Books, 1972), 191.

Chapter 6. The Myth of Overpopulation?

1. Thomas Doubleday, *The True Law of Population* (London: Smith, Elder & Company, 1853), accessed June 26, 2015, http://babel.hathitrust.org/cgi/pt?id=hvd.32044014578611;view=1up,seq=5.

2. White House Office of Policy Development, "US Policy Statement for the International Conference on Population," Population and Development Review 19, no. 3 (September 1948): 574–579, http://www.jstor.org/stable/1973537?seq=1#page_scan_tab_contents.

3. Thomas Robertson, *The Malthusian Moment: Global Population Growth and the Birth of American Environmentalism* (New Brunswick, NJ: Rutgers University Press, 2012), chap. 9: "Ronald Reagan, the New Right and Population Growth."

4. Julian L. Simon, *The Ultimate Resource* (Princeton, NJ: Princeton University Press, 1981), 6–7.

5. Ibid., chap. 22, 7.

6. Ibid., 4.

7. Julian L. Simon, "The *Limits to Growth, Global 2000*, and Their Relatives," *Forecasting Principles*, accessed June 30, 2015, http://www.forecastingprinciples.com/files/Simon%20-%20Limits%20to%20Growth%20AFTERNOTE(1).pdf.

8. Simon, *The Ultimate Resource*, 340.

9. Kingsley Davis, "Will Family Planning Solve the Population Problem?" *The Victor-Bostrum Fund Report for the International Planned Parenthood Federation,*

Report no. 10, Fall 1968, 116. Cited in David Huff, *The Freeman*, Foundation for Economic Education, January 1, 1989, http://fee.org/freeman/detail/freedom-coercion-and-family-size.

10. Simon, *The Ultimate Resource*, 341.

11. "Total Fertility Rate," *Eurostat*, accessed July 1, 2015, http://ec.europa.eu/eurostat/tgm/table.do?tab=table&init=1&language=en&pcode=tsdde220&plugin=1.

12. "Fertility Rate, Total (Births per Woman)," *The World Bank*, accessed July 1, 2015, http://data.worldbank.org/indicator/SP.DYN.TFRT.IN.

13. "World Population to 2300," Economic & Social Affairs, United Nations, 2004, Figure 33, http://www.un.org/esa/population/publications/longrange2/WorldPop2300final.pdf.

14. "A Generation of One-Child Families?" *The Futurist*, June 1985, 49, and Fred Pearce, "Welcome to the Global Old Folks' Home," *New Scientist*, July 9, 1987, 33–34.

15. Ben Wattenberg, *The Birth Dearth* (New York: Pharos Books, 1987), 13.

16. Ibid., 107.

17. Ibid., 114.

Chapter 7. The Consequences of Overpopulation

1. "Table 1. Wheat: Planted Acerage, Harvested Acerage, Production, Yield, and Farm Price," United States Department of Agriculture. Economic Research Service, August 12, 2015, http://www.ers.usda.gov/datafiles/Wheat_Wheat_Data/Yearbook_Tables/US_Acreage_Production_Yield_and_Farm_Price/wheatyearbook table01full.pdf.

2. Lester Brown, "The Grain Drain," *The Futurist*, July/August 1989, 10.

3. Peter Hendry, "Food and Population: Beyond Five Billion," *Population Bulletin*, April 1988, 5.

4. Julian L. Simon, *The Ultimate Resource* (Princeton, NJ: Princeton University Press, 1981), 58.

5. W. Jackson Davis, *The Seventh Year: Industrial Civilization in Transition* (New York: W. W. Norton, 1979), 189.

6. *New York Times*, August 28, 1977, A11, as quoted in Simon, 64.

7. "Towards a New Green Revolution," Food and Agriculture Organization, accessed July 2, 2015, http://www.fao.org/docrep/x0262e/x0262e06.htm.

8. Lester Brown et al., *State of the World-1989* (New York: W. W. Norton, 1989), 43.

9. Kenneth E. Maxwell, Greayer Mansfield-Jones, and Dorothy Mansfield-Jones, *Environment of Life*, 4th ed. (Monterey, CA: Brooks/Cole, 1985), 121.

10. Werner Fornos, "Population Politics," *Technology Review*, February/March 1991, 43.

11. Hendry, 26.

12. Brown, 42.

13. Ibid.

14. Ibid., 55

15. Ibid., 13

16. U. N. Food and Agriculture Organization, *FAO Production Yearbook*, (Rome: n.d.), cited in Brown, 1989, 14.

17. "The Threat of Population Growth," *World Press Review*, August 1987, 58.

18. Simon, *The Ultimate Resource*, 5.

19. David W. Hopper, "The Development of Agriculture in Developing Countries," *Scientific American*, September 1976, 201.

20. Julian L. Simon and Herman Kahn, eds. *The Resourceful Earth* (Oxford, England: Basil Blackwell, 1984), 95.

21. Simon, *The Ultimate Resource*, 5.

22. Simon and Kahn, 192–193.

23. Ibid., 99–100.

24. Steve Connor, "Overpopulation is 'Main Threat to Planet'," *The Independent*, January 7, 2006, http://www.independent.co.uk/environment/overpopulation-is-main-threat-to-planet-521925.html.

25. Nafis Sadik, "The State of the World Population 1988" (New York: United Nations Population Fund, n.d.), 2.

26. Donella H. Meadows, Dennis L. Meadows, Jorgen Randers, and William W. Behrens III, *The Limits to Growth* (New York: Universe Books, 1972), 56–59.

27. For example, see Davis, 128–129.

28. Gerald Barney, *The Global 2000 Report* (New York: Pergamon Press, 1980), 1.

29. For an Optimist's review of *Global 2000*, see Simon and Kahn, chap 1.

30. Simon, The Ultimate Resource, 6, 95–99.

31. David McClintick and Ross B. Emmett, "Betting on the Wealth of Nature: The Simon-Ehrlich Water," *PERC Report* 23, no. 3 (Fall 2005), http://www.perc .org/articles/betting-wealth-nature.

32. Brown, 2–3; Sadik., 8–11.

33. Brown, 60.

34. Sadik, 8.

35. Simon, *The Ultimate Resource*, 82.

36. Ibid., 83.

37. Ibid., 242–243.

38. Simon and Kahn, 451.

39. Simon, *The Ultimate Resource*, chap. 17.

40. National Research Council, *Population Growth and Economic Development: Policy Questions* (Washington, DC: National Academy Press, 1986), 39.

41. Peter Passell, "Economists Start to Fret Again About Population," *New York Times*, December 18, 1990, C1.

42. Thomas Malthus, *An Essay on the Principle of Population* (London: J. Johnson, 1798), 5, http://www.esp.org/books/malthus/population/malthus.pdf.

43. Kingsley Davis, "Progress, Poverty, and Population," *Society*, March/April 1988, 4.

44. Brown, 188.

45. John Tierney, "Fanisi's Choice," *Science 86*, January/February 1986, 39.

46. See, for example, the series of articles on population in the special issue of the *Bulletin of the Atomic Scientists*, April 1986.

47. Robert McNamara, "Time Bomb or Myth: The Population Problem," *Foreign Affairs*, Summer 1984, 1118–1119.

48. Fornos, 44

49. Julian Simon, *Theory of Population and Economic Growth* (Oxford, England: Basil Blackwell, 1986).

50. National Research Council, 90.

51. Samuel H. Preston, "Population Growth and Economic Development," *Environment*, March 1986, 33.

52. "Fertility Rate, Total (Births per Woman)," *World Bank*, accessed July 1, 2015, http://data.worldbank.org/indicator/SP.DYN.TFRT.IN?display=default.

53. "International Energy Statistics," U.S. Energy Information Administration, accessed July 1, 2015, http://www.eia.gov/cfapps/ipdbproject/IEDIndex3 .cfm?tid=2&pid=2&aid=2.

54. Paul A. Murtaugh and Michael A. Schlax, "Reproduction and the Carbon Legacies of Individuals," *Global Climate Change* (2009), 18, http://www.biological diversity.org/programs/population_and_sustainability/pdfs/OSUCarbon Study.pdf.

55. Jason Plautz, "The Climate-Change Solution No One Will Talk about," *The Atlantic*, November 1, 2014, http://www.theatlantic.com/health/archive/2014/11/ the-climate-change-solution-no-one-will-talk-about/382197/.

Chapter 8. One Solution: Population Control?

l. John Tierney, "Fanisi's Choice," *Science* 86, January/February 1986, 28.

2. Pranay Gupte, *The Crowded Earth: People and the Politics of Population* (New York: W. W. Norton, 1984), 68, 69.

3. G. Tyler Miller Jr., *Living in the Environment*, 4th ed. (Belmont, CA: Wadsworth, 1985), 111.

4. William Petersen, *Population*, 3rd ed. (New York: Macmillan, 1975), 412.

5. Ibid, 743.

6. Fred Pearce, "Welcome to the Global Old Folks' Home," *New Scientist*, July 9, 1987, 33.

GLOSSARY

absolute poverty—A condition of life so characterized by malnutrition, illiteracy, and disease as to be beneath any reasonable definition of human decency.

antinatalist—Describing any effort made to slow population growth.

census—An official enumeration of the population with details of age, sex, occupation, marital status, etc. conducted by the government.

civilization—An advanced state of society in which a high level of culture, science, industry, and government have been reached.

climate change—A change in weather patterns for an extended period of time.

demography—The science of vital and social statistics of a population (birth, death, disease, marriage, etc.).

disease—Any abnormal condition that causes the body to malfunction; illness.

emigration—To leave one country in order to settle in another.

epidemic—A temporary prevalence of a disease.

famine—Extreme scarcity of food in a large area.

immigration—To come to a country of which one is not a native, usually for permanent residence.

incentive—Something that brings about action or greater effort as a reward for increased productivity or a job well done.

internal migration—Moving to another location within the same country or region.

LDCs (less developed countries)—Nations with relatively lower standards of living.

MDCs (more developed countries)—Nations that have a relatively high standard of living.

natural resources—The natural wealth of a country including land, forests, mineral deposits, water, agriculture, etc.

optimist—A person or group that tends to look at circumstances in a more favorable light.

overpopulation—An excessive number of people, usually in reference to straining resources, facilities, and economics.

pandemic—Prevalent throughout an entire country, continent, or the whole world.

pessimist—A person or group that tends to look at circumstances in a less favorable light.

population—The total number of persons inhabiting an area.

population control—The practice of artificially altering the size of a population.

pronatalist—In favor of birth; describing any effort made to increase birth rate.

resources—The collective wealth of a country.

total fertility rate (TFR)—The average number of children that would be born to a female over her lifetime.

urbanization—When a rural area takes on the characteristics of a city (such as crowding, increased population, and pollution).

zero population growth (ZPG)—The state of a country or other area when the number of births and deaths is equal and there is no change in the population.

FOR MORE INFORMATION

Do Something.org

www.dosomething.org

A website that helps teenagers find social projects in which they are interested and that they want to work on.

Population Growth

ciese.org/curriculum/popgrowthproj

This website contains a number of student activities that help teenagers learn more about the basic facts and applications of demography and population topics.

Youth Activism Project

youthactivismproject.org

Suggestions for projects and activities for young adults relating to problems of importance to them.

FURTHER READING

Andregg, Michael. *Seven Billion and Counting: The Crisis in Global Population Growth*. Minneapolis: Twenty-First Century Books, 2014.

Barber, Nicola. *Coping with Population Growth*. Chicago: Raintree, 2011.

Bellamy, Rufus. *Population Growth*. Mankato, MN: Amicus, 2011.

Goldin, Ian. *Is the Planet Full?* Oxford: Oxford University Press, 2014.

Haugen, David M., and Susan Musser. *Population*. Detroit: Greenhaven Press, 2012.

Weeks, John R. *Population: An Introduction to Concepts and Issues*. Belmont, CA: Wadsworth Publishing, 2015.